FIASCOES AND FOIBLES

ISBN: 9798846684744

Fiascoes and Foibles

An Unfiltered Look at Public
Finance, Media, Politics
and Sports

Paul Burton

Contents

Preface

" **F**iascoes and Foibles" is a fitting title for this book. My anecdotal essays reflect largely on public-finance coverage over the final 10 years of my career, against the backdrop of 45 years in media. They capture drama, missteps and intrigue with color and biting, irreverent humor.

"I think we journalists are afforded a special observation post for the strangeness of life and the myriad motivations of the people we cover," a longtime colleague told me when I retired late in 2021.

My career began when I was a teenager in the early 1970s. My first "pay raise" was actually an adjustment to bring my hourly wage up to the federal minimum. It ended with my making sure an employer I distrusted wasn't using December holiday calendar irregularities to shortchange me in my final paycheck. Happily, they paid me in full. The time in between involved a long roller-coaster ride that was variously scintillating, profitable and frustrating.

My opening chapters are about the tumultuous state of media, yesterday and today, and about my experience at trade publication Bond Buyer. Other chapters dwell on some of my favorite coverage, including transportation in New York City, the debt crisis in Harrisburg, Pennsylvania, and the 38 Studios financing fiasco in Rhode Island involving former major-league baseball pitcher Curt Schilling. Interviewing the likes of Richard Ravitch, Gina Raimondo and Rodney Slater was a blast. You'll read plenty about Boston, where it all started for me, and Connecticut, where I spent a formative decade.

Anyone who worked in a newspaper or television newsroom, large or small, can relate to this book. Surely my stance on the shortcomings of "strict constructionist" journalism, or simply staying in your coverage lane, will resonate. I've referred to constantly "punching above our weight" while working at small-to-medium sized media outlets.

Communications and business students may also find this book enlightening, as well as those starting out in public finance or anyone who simply wants to know more about it. Personnel types will take interest in my chapter about the many problems related to open-plan office spaces and work-at-home dynamic variables, while "The Technoid Scourge" is not an older person's rant about technology, but a precautionary tale for all. And while I morphed from sports to business at my career's midpoint, mostly because working too many nights and weekends became a drag, readers will get a glimpse of the role sports played in my career. And you don't have to be in broadcasting or to envision a career in it to enjoy "The Spoken Word." We all speak and listen.

If people with ties to the municipal bond industry read the book because they know me from my coverage of it, then fine. Enjoy it. Just don't expect Bond Buyer 2.0. This book is a fun, provocative read that wields a first-person narrative and mixes deep insight with attitude and sarcasm. These pages are not "safe-space" approved. I throw some sharp elbows, but praise is also there for the deserving.

While I miss the occasional adrenaline rush of media work, I surely don't miss the internal nonsense. I'm doing well in retirement. I sleep late many mornings, spend days at the gym and handle some freelance and consulting assignments. My freelance work has included copy editing a sports book, which was personally rewarding and appropriate given my senior editor and sports backgrounds.

As I promised, I'm not cowering in some senior home playing bridge.

– Paul Burton

Little hair, lots of stomach medicine

A media career is not for the faint of heart

At the end of 2021, I retired as northeast regional editor of the Bond Buyer, wrapping up my 45-year career in full-time journalism. People have been leaving the Bond Buyer and parent company Arizent, formerly SourceMedia, for various reasons. For me, the overwork and the office politics were a bit much.

Besides, when the young woman on the Weather Channel began to look like a 25-year-old Kathy Hochul, I figured it was time to get out.

The Bond Buyer — a national, New York-based business-to-business newspaper and website that covered public finance — wasn't the only media outlet with a conga line heading out the door. People are leaving the industry in droves, and I don't blame them.

"All of us who have been doing this journalism thing for a while know that the reasons include low pay, exhaustion from the screams of haters, brutal work schedules, handcuffing contracts and job insecurity," Al Tompkins of nonprofit media institute Poynter wrote in a commentary. "And journalists tell me they do not get a feeling that their bosses or company care about them."

During my final year at the Bond Buyer, where staff cuts forced journalists to also become graphic artists among other things, I was stretched out covering New York City, Philadelphia, several transit organizations including the Metropolitan Transportation Authority

(MTA), plus nine states. And after I left, regional editors were covering as many as three U.S. regions.

Even before the pandemic, red flags were out there. Distrust of the C-suite level had long festered, notably after the revelation of an internal email sent at performance evaluation time that warned newsroom managers not to write positive reviews, even when warranted, because "we don't want to give out pay raises." Some people went nearly a decade without pay hikes while higher-ups kept getting their bonuses.

Tony Suchon, who hired me as a copy editor at mergers-and-acquisitions oriented financial media company The Deal and whose job as copy chief I later filled after he moved out of town, hated formal evaluations. He smiled at me once and said, "Here's your review: Come back tomorrow." He then wrote the same praiseworthy review, verbatim, for all eight of us in our department, and human resources bought it lock, stock and barrel. Tony bragged about it to us afterward, laughing all the while. His favorite saying? "Don't tell personnel. Don't tell the suits."

SourceMedia once offered me a so-called promotion, but no pay raise came with it, only a suspicious-sounding promise of "we'll take care of you in the next round." That didn't pass the stink test. Further, I would have had to assume full supervisory responsibilities for a co-worker from hell, arguably the most high-maintenance colleague in the history of commerce. The less said about him, the better.

A "promotion" with no raise means your employer places no value on your additional duties.

Sensing the politburo was trying to hose me, in no small part because of my age, I rejected the offer. "Promotions with no pay raises, that's the SourceMedia way," said one grizzled veteran at a sister publication. I relayed to the suits that I considered this a bad business practice. That made me a target. Before long, I got a writeup in my personnel file that falsely accused me of "repeatedly throwing objects at co-workers." I never threw anything at anybody. The author of the letter lectured about being a professional, but his behavior at company conferences was anything but.

Much to the chagrin of the ivory tower, I became the external face of the Bond Buyer. I appeared on national television and radio, gave frequent media interviews and guest-lectured at elite universities and prep schools. People referenced my work in books and scholarly journals. The company's treatment of me, though, was disproportionately negative. Over time I became a gadfly, the in-house Rasputin. I'll admit, though, I fed off the Rasputin schtick.

Changes at the C-suite level occurred later in my tenure. In came a different kind of poison, some self-smitten types with sketchy fad titles that included a "chief people officer" — a goateed hipster who got easily offended — and a "director of research intelligence." In one charade, photos along our corridors showed staffers describing what constituted leadership. Some were functionaries. I can't say exactly how many they dumped once the pandemic took hold.

One year, because of severe cost cutting, the suits had our Washington bureau chief stay in an outer-borough youth hostel when he came up for an awards dinner. Simply refusing to cover the cost of the trip would have been more dignified. Flat-salaried editorial staff, presumably under pressure from above, were promoting company conference registrations on social media: "30% discount, use promo code XYZ," or whatever. I fought off this sort of mission creep. Selling the company's brand was never my job, as I saw it. That's for the marketing people. Pay me a marketing differential and maybe then we'll talk. I'm not an unpaid billboard. Likewise, I would not attend a business luncheon or dinner simply to "wave the banner" for my employer. I would go only for news value or contacts to nurture.

At the end I had very little hair and lots of stomach medicine. But my long and diverse run in the media, while highly stressful, was still fascinating.

Over many years I covered everything from high finance to the National Hockey League, often working for small-to-medium media outlets punching above our weight. Landing the occasional knockout punch was especially satisfying. As a Boston native, for example, I took great pride in scooping the hometown Globe and Herald, which I grew up reading, with a Bond Buyer story about the financially problematic MBTA Retirement Fund, the public pension fund for Greater Boston's mass transit workers. And as a senior-level editor, an editor-in-chief of a sports magazine and, at multiple places, a newspaper sports editor, I helped shape many careers. I worked people hard, but I was actually easy to work for. If you gave me an honest effort and didn't play games, I stood behind you. Give me attitude, and I'd give it back in triplicate.

It was also a privilege to spend my last 20 years or so working in financial journalism in New York City, including my stretch as senior editor and copy chief at The Deal. Not bad for a blue-collar kid from Boston. The Deal by far was my best employer. They paid us well and treated us well, and as a startup, we threw down a marker for creative enterprise business news. The best piece I edited was Matt Miller's cover story about Detroit's woes, which nicely veered from the standard mergers and acquisitions fare while still resonating with that business-to-business publication's readers. Miller was the gold standard for long-form writing.

I inherited the copy chief's job there from two excellent predecessors, and despite our having to process more print and online publications with the same staff, our well-edited products got out on time. My copy editors were in the good-to-excellent range, although I inherited my share of drama queens and clubhouse lawyers. One of them, a dour sort who majored in museum studies, had anxieties about working on deadline. Some people in our business shit the bed under pressure. I kept him away from our quick-turnaround daily products and gave him weekly magazine material, where he was useful. Still, you don't want to hire anyone with an arts background for a deadline-heavy job.

When The Deal eliminated my position and some others in 2009, shortly after the death of our sugar daddy, corporate dealmaker Bruce Wasserstein, I got a decent severance package and was able to clear out my desk in predawn privacy. No security thugs peered over my shoulder.

Even as media became more digitized — a chapter in this book will cover tech's alarming influence on the industry — the culture too often remained in the Dark Ages: all stick, no carrot. No good deed went unpunished. One place I worked in Connecticut defined a "vacation" as essentially a favor they were doing us so we could come back and run the treadmill faster after we got our rest. There, a burned-out editorial leader invoked the militaristic phrase "chain of command." Many personnel experts call such usage a red flag.

Recent ownership by the latest wave of bad guys — private-equity and hedge-fund folks who'll kill you for a quarter — has clearly hurt the industry. To call these people snakes would offend serpents.

"Hedge-fund ownership is one of, if not *the*, worst developments that have occurred for newspapers," media columnist Margaret Sullivan said in a New York Times interview. "These companies don't care about journalism. They care about strip-mining what's left for whatever profits can be squeezed, not with an eye to a sustainable future but with an eye toward next quarter's balance sheet." Sullivan is a former public editor of the Times and was the first woman to serve as the top editor of the Buffalo News.

Recently and sadly, I canceled my subscription to Sports Illustrated magazine, which I had received since my teen years in the late 1960s. SI was a role model as I began in sports journalism, which encompassed roughly the first half of my career. As the editor-in-chief of Hartford Sports Extra magazine in Connecticut in the mid-to-late 1980s, I strove to make it the "Sports Illustrated of Greater Hartford." But SI changed for the worse. Late in 2019, new ownership, or as Dennis Young of the New York Daily News put it, "notorious media goons Ross Levinsohn and James Heckman," gutted the SI staff, cutting up to 40 people. "Sports Illustrated might be legendary, but there's nothing more cutting-edge in modern media than getting destroyed by cheap hacks who don't care about the product," Young wrote.

Alden Global Capital's purchase in 2021 of Tribune Publishing, a newspaper chain that includes the Hartford Courant, triggered a reaction from Hartford Mayor Luke Bronin. "A strong Hartford Courant is a vital to our community and vital to a healthy, strong democracy here in Connecticut," Bronin said. "I am deeply concerned by this takeover because this hedge fund's record is clear, and it is not good."

Alden, in 2011, bought what was arguably the nastiest newspaper group of all, the Journal Register Company (JRC) of Trenton, New Jersey. I bolted upstate New York when JRC and its tyrannical chief executive, Robert Jelenic, took over the Daily Freeman in Kingston, where I was sports editor. JRC actually did me a favor. News of their pending arrival gave me the kick in the ass I needed to leave a place I had clearly outgrown.

"Checking odometers in reporters' cars against expense reports, running front-page ads and compelling publishers to promptly send weekly financial reports so Jelenic can scan for the odd indulgence are traditions at Journal Register," Nathan Vardi wrote in Forbes magazine.

As I left Kingston, Jelenic was insisting on full box scores with Little League baseball results, akin to Yankees and Mets major-league coverage. We had to insist on this from barely literate coaches who had trouble spelling their own kids' names correctly. On the day Jelenic signed off on the newspaper purchase, I was in New Jersey accepting a job offer. Delightful timing.

Jelenic was known to fire personnel, including the publisher of the New Haven Register, during face-to-face meetings on airport tarmacs. He also called for instant dismissals if a paper missed its weekly revenue target. It could be any employee, didn't matter who, no severance. "It was an extremely hostile environment," Gerald Ryerson, who quit as the Register's chief financial officer, told Mary Walton in an American Journalism Review article. "If you did a forecast and the answer wasn't what top management — meaning Bob — wanted … You know the story about 'Don't shoot the messenger'? The messenger would get shot."

Reporters that requested new notebooks had to prove the previous ones were filled. Jelenic's micromanaging also included determining which writer within his group of Connecticut newspapers would cover the Hartford Whalers hockey team.

"I've never dealt with a newspaper company that was so paranoid," said Walton, a former Philadelphia Inquirer reporter.

I also worked for two years at the Gannett-owned Daily Record in Parsippany, New Jersey. Gannett, which foisted locator maps and "how-to" boxes on readers, was also a micromanager. When you designed a page, you wondered what about it would trigger a memo from corporate headquarters in Virginia. While interviewing for a sports editor opening at a Gannett paper in Utica, New York, in the late 1990s, I saw a convoluted design for the lead sports page. I asked the assistant sports editor about that page, and he said in so many words that Gannett wouldn't let him do A, B and C, so he did D, E and F. And then there was the self-flagellating memo you had to write when a Gannett newspaper published a correction that was on you. You had to "explain your thoughts," and simply saying you screwed up — we've all done that — was not enough. It created a mistake trail supervisors could use during evaluations. I left Parsippany in the nick of time. A new executive editor worked people to the bone and dismissively told staff they were lucky to be working for the biggest newspaper chain in America. Gannett today is a shell of its old self.

Journalists always had updated resumes handy, with many having a few in the mail — or in later years, the email. Back when Editor & Publisher magazine was a must-read because of its many help-wanted ads, newsroom managers would engage in the petty practice of hiding the magazine from the rest of us. No problem. We subscribed to it at home.

In her final speech as a member of the New York MTA board, Veronica Vanterpool, now a deputy administrator with the Federal Transit Administration, praised all of local transit media as dogged, thorough and accurate. We looked at each other in the media room at MTA headquarters and agreed that we never heard such praise from within our own companies.

Beyond bonds

*Go wide with news coverage and reap
the dividends*

At a Bond Buyer conference in my native Boston, a municipal bond analyst saw my name tag and approached me.

"I enjoy your material because it has some bite to it," he said. "Sadly, many in business news aren't like that. They probably think it's not proper."

Business journalism needn't be stuffy, and being "proper" doesn't cut it anymore. The days of Irving R. Levine are gone. Levine, a long-time NBC News business correspondent, reported on monetary policy in the 1970s with a distinctive monotone while clad in a bowtie. His middle initial was part of his signoff. Levine, while accomplished, epitomized the financial news dullness of the time.

The Bond Buyer's regional beat enabled me to be creative. It made for a great run there, despite the company-induced agita I've referenced in this book. I led the charge in covering not only the municipal bond industry but also the wider sphere of public finance, often with an unorthodox bent. "You always find the most interesting angles in our arcane business," a trusted and valued colleague told me. "Keep blazing a trail that the rest of us can follow!"

I was the Bond Buyer's real innovator, and I didn't need any contrived job title.

Unlike staff who covered daily markets activity, I wasn't beholden to yield curves, outflows and the like. I admired how some of our markets people could churn out daily copy about trading volume without their brains turning to mush. My advice to younger people starting out in financial media: Don't drown in numbers.

"There's only so much you can write about a fucking yield curve," said one prominent New York bond lawyer.

I didn't cover just "munis." I stretched the parameters and enjoyed setting a tone that said you can't just cover municipal bond sales until the cows come home. That helped my bottom line as well. My creative work appealed to more people beyond our core readership, and the visibility helped land me some extra freelance side gigs. Thankfully, editor-in-chief Mike Scarchilli gave me full rein and didn't micromanage. I always functioned best as a quasi-independent city-state. If I wanted to go out of town and do a sit-down interview with a governor, I just went. Scarchilli didn't tell me to go cover some dreadful trade association luncheon speech instead.

I often circumvented wonky bond angles in public-finance stories involving budgets, infrastructure, unfunded pension liability and governance to make them more readable without compromising detail. Business news is complicated enough as it is. Why make it more so? Scarchilli considered me especially adept at explaining complex subject matter in plain English and shaping "far-out" story topics for our readership, much like a baseball catcher framing a pitch to make it appear in the strike zone.

"You were the best narrative journalist we had on staff," Scarchilli said.

I made the Bond Buyer fun to read — no small achievement. Outside-the-box coverage included how COVID-19 changed the fight for street space in New York City; the untapped potential of commuter rail as an inner-city transit option in New York, Boston and elsewhere; controversy over bus-hub relocation plans at Kennedy Plaza in downtown Providence, Rhode Island; and the fierce debate over automated-vehicle use in Pittsburgh. All related to public finance and were highly relevant to our readers.

Strange as it sounds, given the name of our publication, force-feeding the bond angle sometimes watered down a good story. Our readers were smart enough to detect artificial prose when they saw it. Besides, our readers were attuned to the world at large, not just the municipal bond bubble. For example, we factored commuter context into our coverage of New York MTA finances. After all, many of our high-end readers were commuters, too, whether they traipsed by subway along the Upper East Side or by rail from Long Island, Westchester County or New Jersey.

We even added colorful twists to our mainstream coverage. A feature about New York City subway infrastructure needs included a link to the infamous "pizza rat" video, which went viral on social media and showed a large rodent carrying a pizza slice down a subway staircase. News about the Massachusetts Bay Transportation Authority, which operated Greater Boston mass transit, would sometimes link the Kingston Trio's 1959 hit folk song about a fictional character who rode the Boston subways, got lost and never returned.

I launched a New York City Hall bureau, with senior markets reporter Chip Barnett available for periodic backup. And my northeast regional partner, Andrew Coen, was solid. I always thought that beyond his heavyweight beats of New Jersey, New York State and Philadelphia, Andrew's coverage of colleges, counties and smaller cities provided important pieces of our editorial puzzle and proof that pageviews aren't a be-all and end-all. He is now doing well for the Commercial Observer, a real estate–oriented trade publication. My regional peers included some high-quality people: Yvette Shields in Chicago, Keeley Webster in Los Angeles, Richard Williamson in Texas and Shelly Sigo in Florida. Separately, I liked the unheralded work Aaron Weitzman did on the markets side, even though we never really worked together directly. He now covers private equity for the media outlet PE Hub.

Bond ratings were part of our bread-and-butter coverage, and I had some excellent capital-markets commentators at my disposal: Howard Cure, Alan Schankel, Tom Kozlik, Natalie Cohen and John Ceffalio come to mind. I deepened our bullpen with additional talking heads, often by subject matter: They included Nicole Gelinas on New York infrastructure; Alan Rubin on climate; John Boyd Jr. on corporate relocation; Bob Boland and Lee Igel on sports management and financing; David Fiorenza on Pennsylvania and New Jersey; and Gary Sasse on Rhode Island. In New York City, watchdog groups Citizens Budget Commission and the Independent Budget Office provided valuable insights.

I tended to sidestep direct interviews with bond-rating agency folks because their comments were too close to the vest, and they often just regurgitated reports. Never go to a rating analyst if you want a good quote. Still, I had my favorites among them: Eric Kim, Doug Offerman and Amy Laskey from Fitch; and David Hitchcock and Tiffany Tribbitt from S&P. I got a kick out of my one-on-one chat with Jules Kroll right after his namesake investigations firm entered the municipal ratings market. Kroll made a niche for himself chasing down assets belonging to the likes of reviled Iraqi President Saddam Hussein. Midway through the interview with me, Kroll interrupted himself and said, "That's a strange way you take notes." The super-sleuth was eyeballing my note-taking.

Internal headwinds included some desk editors who tried to weaken vibrant prose by deleting colorful quotes, adding excess data and inserting the dreaded passive voice. The late Associated Press editor Rene J. Cappon, in his book "The Word," railed against these kinds of practices, which he labeled "genteelism," or the use of lame words and phrases just to be polite. "Expressed concern" is such an example. Cliched headlines, meanwhile, spoke of "paradigm shifts" and "game changers."

Desk personnel included a deadweight whose executive editor title was inflated. He was an upper-management plant who thought he was the brightest guy in the room because he once worked for Bloomberg News. He didn't last at Bloomberg, but that didn't stop him from referring to our staff as "so-called journalists." He also disparaged southerners, mocked how they spoke and said the decline of the English language began when the banking industry moved from San Francisco to Charlotte, North Carolina. Another desk jockey on the West Coast considered MTA news irrelevant. Never mind that we cover the debt markets and the MTA carries about $50 billion in debt. I also wished I had a dollar for every time he used "seen as" in a headline.

Late in my Bond Buyer run, Scarchilli clarified that second-day angles were more important than breaking news. We simply didn't have the staffing levels that Bloomberg or the Wall Street Journal did to corner the breaking stuff, but we had — at least at the time — a solid core of media-savvy people who knew the industry and could follow up with material on what was really behind the breaking story. At a staff meeting, I praised the move but warned against in-house overuse of the word "analytical," which could prompt waves of tedious copy that would read like a bond-rating report from Moody's.

I was always the push-the-envelope type. "Core mission" to me represented stagnation. As sports editor at a chain of Hartford-area newspapers very early in my career, I went to the Bronx on the sly and interviewed the legendary "voice of Yankee Stadium," Bob Sheppard. The interview was half about the Yankees and half about the decline of English-language usage. Sheppard was a speech professor at St. John's University. The publisher, a Yankee fan, enjoyed the writeup but then gave me a smarmy "stick to your knitting" lecture about local news priorities. I didn't tell the publisher that resume-padding was my primary motivation for the Sheppard piece, but he probably sensed that.

On the local cable station, we didn't stop with high school sporting events. My studio guests included Emile Francis, general manager of the National Hockey League's Hartford Whalers and Chet Simmons, the president of then-fledgling ESPN who's best known as the mastermind behind ABC's acclaimed "Wide World of Sports" series.

In upstate New York I staffed a season-opening high school football game between Coxsackie-Athens, in the far fringe of the Kingston-based Daily Freeman's circulation area, and Albany-area school Watervliet, a two-time defending state champion whose head coach, Dan Reinfurt, committed suicide one month earlier. His death generated a cover package on USA Today's lead page. I assigned that game to get a human-interest angle on what had become a national story. My writer, Evan Margulies, did a compelling follow-up, having overheard a pregame, read-the-riot-act speech by Reinfurt's successor to his players. This was beyond our core readership, beyond football, beyond wins and losses. We went outside our lane and rightly so.

Colorful, historic context can also enrich. As NYC Health + Hospitals looks to recraft itself, let's not forget the fiasco during the 1980s when Victor Botnick, a whiz kid working with a phony resume in Mayor Ed Koch's administration, briefly ran the municipal hospital system. What's coverage of fixing the aged Brooklyn-Queens Expressway without reference to the city's imperious uber-commissioner of yesteryear, Robert Moses? Likewise, parking revenue news within the five boroughs evokes memories of former Bronx Democratic leader Stanley Friedman and the Parking Violations Bureau scandal.

A piece about the new cross-border bridge connecting Detroit to Windsor, Ontario, would be incomplete without references to the politics surrounding the existing, privately run Ambassador Bridge and its eccentric owner, the late Matty Moroun. His Byzantine land holdings in Detroit interweaved with any discussion about the city's bankruptcy and attempted recovery. And in Pennsylvania a parade of corruption at the state level triggered memories of Budd Dwyer, the state treasurer who killed himself at his own press conference, following his pay-to-play conviction.

"The reason you're good at what you do is that you go out there. People know you," one colleague said. News doesn't come to you through press releases from coiffed people in a pristine conference room with a sailboat painting on the wall. Go to Wilkes-Barre, Pennsylvania, a throwback to the coal-industry days of yesteryear, with a newsstand named "Anthracite" sitting around the corner from Coal Avenue. Then attend a City Council hearing about the city's application to the state for special distressed-community status. Or visit New Haven, Connecticut, where the divide between Ivy League Yale University and the rest of the struggling city is palpable. And while you're there, traipse over to neighboring West Haven to explore why that city's such a financial basket case.

The shutdowns from COVID-19 limited me from going out and about during my final months. I felt neutralized. On March 9, 2020, I shuttled between City Hall and MTA headquarters covering budget- and pandemic-related hearings and press conferences, while separately that day, news broke that Rick Cotton, the executive director of the Port Authority of New York and New Jersey, had the coronavirus. Days later everything shut down and Zoom meetings became the order of the day. I did my share of high-quality enterprise stories, including how disasters shaped New York City throughout its history. Mitchell Moss, director of New York University's Rudin Center for Transportation Policy and Management, loved to recite chapter and verse about the city's reactions to previous calamities that included blizzards, the Spanish flu of a century earlier, the Sept. 11 terrorist attacks and the recession of 2008–2009.

Unfortunately, the pandemic gave our higher-ups an excuse to cut further to the bone of editorial staffing. I also noticed over the years a marginalizing of regional news. The desk editors gave my coverage of the scandal prompting New York Gov. Andrew Cuomo's resignation the witness protection treatment, placing it on the website where few people would see it. Office politics factored in, I'm sure, because the stories were mine. But that was brutally shortsighted, to say the least. We cover the public sector, and Cuomo, especially during the pandemic, was arguably the most visible U.S. governor.

The Bond Buyer's home page, meanwhile, kept displaying smiling faces of industry regulators, notably Emily Brock of the Government Finance Officers Association and Leslie Norwood of the Securities Industry and Financial Markets Association — or as one former colleague groused, "The same people you see in the Bond Buyer every five minutes." Brock even remarked to our Washington bureau that her photo was running too often. Brock and Norwood are highly respected for their work, but the photo overkill was silly.

As I left, coverage included over-the-top cheerleading for environmental, social and governance (ESG) practices. The Bond Buyer wasn't alone in this. The ESG phenomenon across various media drew the wrath of veteran business journalist Charlie Gasparino, who decried it as a "woke investor fad." Gasparino, a Fox News commentator and New York Post columnist, called ESG "an amorphous group of edicts that have been adopted by big Wall Street firms, investment managers and many corporations to allegedly make the world a better place. Follow ESG edicts and you will help protect the environment by investing in windmills instead of oil companies. ... You can virtue signal 'til the cows come home despite obvious drawbacks."

ESG admittedly is a rising and contentious factor in public finance, and many of us are curious about whether bond-rating agencies will factor municipal corruption — in Chicago, for instance — into ratings. "If they are serious about the 'G' in 'ESG,' [they] will factor systemic corruption into their ratings," said Greg Clark, head of municipal research at Debtwire, a capital markets–oriented media company.

The only thing good about my final year at the Bond Buyer was racking up Social Security credit for working extra months past full retirement. My work remained high-quality because I had a strong personal brand to uphold. Operating at home did enable me to function off the radar, not that I didn't in normal times. I used coded Latin dummy text in my story drafts in our editing system to keep others from knowing what I was working on. Some of the files were possible side-gig material. In addition, I capped my weekly hours and column inches, akin to a baseball pitcher on a pitch-count limit. On Fridays I flipped the switch to freelance at some point or just called it a day. "Maxed out on hours and column inches" was my pro-forma email reply.

The Bond Buyer began 2022 terribly shorthanded, not unlike many other media outlets. People of substance are mostly retired or have gone elsewhere, and I feel for the legacy folks that do remain.

While I didn't miss the office, I missed being "out there," mingling with news sources and other media. Those people made it all worthwhile.

Of trains and daddies

New York MTA can't stand clear of the sharp-elbow politics

In June 2018, five months into his presidency of the MTA's New York City Transit Division, Andy Byford held a town hall meeting at John Jay High School in Brooklyn's Park Slope neighborhood, where pedestrians dodge hipster moms pushing baby carriages the size of Sherman tanks.

"One thing I've learned in my long career is never to get into politics as best I can," Byford told one public speaker.

Local transit advocates embraced the effervescent Byford as the "Train Daddy." He had modernized systems in London, Sydney and Toronto and set out to do the same in New York. "This guy's flying high coming into New York," said Emmett Adler, who directed "End of the Line," an independent film about the MTA.

But Byford's initiatives, whether he wanted them or not, were deep into politics. Early in 2020, Byford had had enough. Tired of interference from the meddlesome Gov. Andrew Cuomo, he resigned as chief of NYC Transit, the MTA's subway-and-bus unit.

Byford loved the media. And news coverage made him a celebrity of sorts. The CBS magazine show "60 Minutes" profiled him. Local newscasts showed him picking up trash, riding with conductors and pushing a broom to clear excessive water from flooded stations, all while decked out in a suit. Media warmed to his British vernacular, which included a "villain train" to describe a broken-down car hitched to the others. The day he introduced his "Fast Forward" modernization plan, he stuck his head into the media room at MTA headquarters, smiled and yelled out, "Hi, everybody!" And when frequent public speaker Jason Anthony Piniero referenced his own birthday at a board meeting, Byford obliged with a gift — an autographed copy of Fast Forward.

On his last day at the job, on Feb. 21, 2020, Byford left MTA headquarters on 2 Broadway in Lower Manhattan to a chorus of cheers in the crowded lobby and outside. The MTA's inner workings resonate with the millions of everyday New Yorkers who ride the system and must cope with its headaches.

Two weeks later, and days after a handful of us from transit media and advocacy groups joined Byford for an informal goodbye party at nearby Murphy's tavern, WCBS-Ch.2 aired an interview with him.

"Largely it was just sheer frustration toward the end of my tenure," he said. "I thought that the job had become somewhat intolerable. I felt myself somewhat marginalized. … My people were being directed behind my back."

Cuomo wore the black hat. The media saw Cuomo, the son of the late Gov. Mario Cuomo, as jealous of the attention Byford received. Cuomo controlled the MTA and its board with such a grip that Veronica Vanterpool, then a city-appointed board member and later a deputy administrator with the Federal Transit Administration, once said her peers felt "neutered." Cuomo's heavy-handedness included tastelessly making fun of former MTA chairman Tom Prendergast's weight in front of the media.

"Byford's growing presence as the face of the subways clearly got under Cuomo's notoriously thin skin," Steve Cuozzo wrote in the New York Post. Cuomo's reaction when Byford quit was terse. "He stays, he leaves, nothing changes," he told reporters.

"I didn't seek the moniker of 'Train Daddy.' I didn't seek publicity," Byford told Ch. 2. "But a good transit professional gets out and about. You can't run a transit system from a desk."

Byford shortly thereafter returned to Britain where he is commissioner of Transport for London. Instead of grappling with Cuomo,

Byford was guiding Queen Elizabeth — four months before her death — on a tour that marked the completion of London's $22 billion Crossrail construction project. It was renamed the Elizabeth Line in honor of the queen. New York media followed up on that event, proving how Byford's all-too-brief stay at the MTA still resonates, even amid the COVID-19 pandemic, worsening crime, skyrocketing inflation and the Russia-Ukraine conflict. Byford also oversees road and taxi systems in his new gig and has suggested that New York would benefit from such an integrated transit authority.

"Andy Byford is a systems thinker with a vision," said Liam Blank, policy and communications manager for the advocacy group Tri-State Transportation Campaign. "He resisted siloed and reactionary planning, which, of course, is what made him a thorn in Gov. Cuomo's side. Even though his tenure was short, he still left a lasting impact on the MTA, which is still rolling out some priorities [such as bus network redesigns] he put in place. He also welcomed transit advocates and gave us a seat at the table, which made the MTA more transparent and accountable."

Byford chafed over Cuomo's intervention in the repair of the Canarsie Tunnel, which sustained considerable damage from Hurricane Sandy in 2012. The tunnel carries the L subway line between Brooklyn and Lower Manhattan. Pre-pandemic, it drew about 400,000 rides every weekday, connecting Manhattan's Chelsea with Brooklyn's Canarsie and featuring some of the city's trendiest and fastest-growing neighborhoods.

The L-train controversy epitomized the MTA's multiple struggles, according to John Surico, a transit journalist whose work has appeared in the New York Times, Bloomberg News and elsewhere. "You have aging infrastructure, lack of maintenance, the rising specter of climate change and political tension over who's responsible for fixing it [and] who's responsible for paying for it," Surico said in the Adler documentary. Local media coined the phrase "L-pocalypse."

Cuomo called for a streamlined method which, according to engineering deans from Cornell and Columbia universities, would save time and money on the work while averting an originally planned 15-month shutdown of the tunnel. Work was officially completed in April 2020, three months ahead of schedule and $100 million under the projected $500 million cost. Only time, say 50 or 100 years from now, will tell whether the move was right.

In addition, a reorganization plan sought to remove Byford from oversight of capital construction projects, essentially cutting his job in half. The chain of events triggered questions from the media about whether Byford was being sidelined and, contrary to the authority's own acknowledged need to streamline, stood to crowd the MTA's upper-executive levels with new positions, including a chief transformation officer.

"There's this whole thing about how Cuomo doesn't want Andy Byford to have too much power because he doesn't like Byford, but I don't think that's the case," infrastructure expert Nicole Gelinas, a senior fellow with the Manhattan Institute for Policy Research, said at the time. "I think he doesn't want any one person to have too much power. He doesn't want anyone to have leverage over him, the governor."

One TV reporter said Cuomo had "daddy issues," adding: "He thinks he's his father, and he's not."

Cuomo's absurd ways included an overreaction to a New York Post article about subway commuters citing a mosquito problem in summer 2016, notably at Rockefeller Station and amid concerns about the Zika virus. After the piece ran, though, MTA officials had trouble finding standing water in the system, so at Cuomo's insistence they staged a press conference at Whitehall station on the lower tip of Manhattan, which they could shut down while keeping the rest of the system running. The MTA then pumped thousands of gallons of water into the subway pits just so Cuomo could swat mosquitoes along the tracks in front of the TV cameras and further placate his ego.

Political maneuvering surrounding the state-run MTA and the city it serves has gone back generations. The authority operates the city's subways, buses, Long Island Rail Road (LIRR) and Metro-North Railroad commuter lines and several interborough bridges and tunnels.

State-city relations have traditionally been fractious, thus creating a disconnect between the state-run MTA and the city it serves.

"The stubborn fact of public transportation is that 'public' means politics," former MTA chairman Richard Ravitch wrote in his book, "So Much to Do: A Full Life of Business, Politics, and Confronting Fiscal Crises." While Ravitch called his four years running the MTA "the most exhilarating of my life," he also cited worsening relations with the elder Cuomo toward the end of his run at MTA in the early 1980s. "There was no doubt that the fun quotient of the [MTA chairmanship] had been diminished by the governor's inexplicable hostility."

Ravitch, one of New York's most influential power brokers for over half a century, went through the wringer getting state lawmakers in Albany to approve a funding package that created the authority's initial five-year capital program. Ravitch gave predawn tours of decrepit parts of the subway system, including rail yards, to business leaders including David Rockefeller of Chase and Walter Wriston of Citigroup. They, in turn, lobbied Republican leaders in Albany to enact a tax package to backstop the capital plan.

"Citibank was an international institution, and Walter Wriston was not a raving liberal. He was rather conservative politically," Ravitch said on my podcast. "But he cared deeply about New York City."

Foreign corporate ownership makes such engagement a harder sell today.

"That's the challenge to a large degree because not only are people in the business world more international in nature ... [but also] in the '70s, most them owned the premises they occupied," Ravitch said. "Today they're tenants, and the real estate's owned by faceless fiduciaries. Pension funds in Canada, pension funds in Australia or Holland own the property, and the businesses are less local."

Chaos has also surrounded the MTA. In 1982 a man stormed into the lobby of headquarters, then on Madison Avenue in Midtown, saying he wanted to kill Ravitch. The man shot and wounded a security guard. "He recovered, but they never found the shooter," Ravitch wrote in his book. Ravitch wore a 25-pound bulletproof vest during a Fordham Law

School commencement speech in oppressive outdoor humidity. The lobby shooting was not the last attack. In a separate incident, someone else walked into the MTA offices and said he had a personal gift for Ravitch. When police wouldn't let the man pass, he pulled out a knife and stabbed an officer, whose thick wallet helped absorb the knife.

"But I continued to function, despite the lack of privacy and the occasional bad dream," Ravitch wrote.

Ravitch, an independent thinker and to some an irritant, was a New York public service Mr. Fix-It for years. "He's a modern-day Cincinnatus who works for the common good without personal ambition," Howard Cure, director of municipal research for Evercore Wealth Management, said while introducing a Ravitch talk.

Best known for his work alongside Felix Rohatyn and others during the city's emergence from its fiscal crisis, Ravitch was in the office with Gov. Hugh Carey in 1975 when banking leaders chillingly said they would no longer underwrite the city's bonds and notes, putting New York on the cusp of bankruptcy.

Ravitch's leadership reverberates today.

"Where is our Felix Rohatyn, where is our Dick Ravitch, where is our Al Shanker right now that we need?" MTA board member Neal Zuckerman said in August 2020, as the authority was deep in its COVID-19 fiscal woes. Shanker, as president of the United Federation of Teachers, agreed in 1975 to purchase $150 million of city bonds from its pension system to help the city out of its crisis.

"The businesses, the municipal governments, the real estate owners who have benefited for decades by our growth, the unions both directly through their wages and through their pensions, the bondholders, the banks … we have many people, many constituencies that came together in 1975 to save the city," said Zuckerman, a senior partner and managing director in the New York office of Boston Consulting Group and a guest on my podcast series.

MTA board meetings were often colorful.

In 2019, board members Larry Schwartz, a former chief of staff to Cuomo, and John Samuelsen, international president of Transport

Workers Union International, shouted at each other during repeated meetings about overtime abuse. A 61-page report by law firm Morrison & Foerster said the cost and management of overtime at the MTA spiraled out of control under leadership's noses for roughly a decade.

The two continued to argue over who was to blame and, according to the website Politico, nearly came to blows during a closed-door executive session. Schwartz called for an independent prosecutor following a report by Albany-based think tank Empire Center for Public Policy that a "chief measurement officer" at LIRR made $300,000 in overtime alone. Samuelsen accused Schwartz of "ranting and raving [on CBS News] in an inappropriate, hyperbolic manner about fraud and abuse among transit workers."

Police arrested a fare-hike protester in December 2008 after he threatened to hurl his shoe at MTA chief executive Elliot Sander. "This shoe's for you," he told Sander right before the board passed a doomsday annual budget with steep fare hikes and service cuts. The suspect, Stephen Millies, said the Iraqi reporter who threw his shoe at President George W. Bush inspired him.

In 2012, MTA chairman Joe Lhota and board member Chuck Moerdler sparred during a debate over the authority's meeting schedule. Lhota wanted to hold fewer meetings and some of them out in the communities. Moerdler, an octogenarian whose affected speech patterns resembled those of John Houseman's old-world character in the movie "The Paper Chase," chided Lhota about the need for better transparency. That set off Lhota, who called Moerdler's comments "scurrilous" and even invoked a dispute concerning Moerdler's alleged use of his police-issued MTA parking placard to park in front of the Cornell Club in Midtown Manhattan for four hours.

"Enough of lying to this board. Be a man. Let's go," said Lhota.

"I will bring it on," said Moerdler. "With respect, I find your comments disturbing."

Lhota replied: "Respect is not mutual."

MTA media-relations staff replayed the exchange for reporters in the video room.

At the press conference following the meeting, Lhota apologized. "My Bronx upbringing came out," he said.

Moerdler, a Holocaust survivor who grew up in Europe, also had a spirited 2015 debate with fellow board member Jonathan Ballan over a ban on political advertising, prompted by anti-Islamic ads placed on buses and subway stations by Pamela Geller from the pro-Israeli advocacy group American Freedom Defense Initiative.

In a highly emotional 10-minute statement, Moerdler advocated the ad restrictions, which passed on a 9-2 vote. He called inflammatory speech "filth" and "garbage" and warned about the perils of such speech unfettered. "'Mein Kampf' was a precursor to genocide," he said, referring to Adolf Hitler's manifesto. "Hateful speech is not harmless speech. Only a fool or a rogue would suggest otherwise."

Ballan, however, warned that the MTA, which had lost three related lawsuits, could find itself on the wrong side of court action again. "This contravenes good public policy, probably is unconstitutional and makes no sense," he said. "Whenever we vary from pure transportation policy, we as a board do not have the expertise and we make errors, and this is just another example of that."

Great back-and-forth stuff. Moerdler and Ballan presented their arguments well.

Several years later the MTA found itself in another crisis, though not of its making: COVID-19. Ridership on subways, buses and commuter rail plummeted about 90% as the city went into lockdown mode and MTA revenue tanked. Chairman Patrick Foye invoked phrases "fiscal tsunami" and "four-alarm fire," among others.

"I don't think I can adequately express what the pandemic did to this organization," Sarah Feinberg, NYC Transit president after Byford, said tearfully in Adler's film. "We have all lost friends; we have all lost colleagues." Roughly 175 MTA workers died from the virus. Feinberg, before she resigned in the summer of 2021, became the face of the MTA in its continued sparring with City Hall, holding the floor in frequent criticisms of then-Mayor Bill de Blasio. Feinberg once turned down Cuomo's offer for her to oversee the entire MTA, citing family priorities.

Federal rescue aid arrived to help prop up the MTA while the authority was able to borrow money through the Municipal Liquidity Facility, an emergency short-term program the Federal Reserve Bank established early in the pandemic. But the MTA may run out of its federal money sooner than it expected because ridership hasn't returned at predicted levels.

Rising crime in the subway system and elsewhere in the city brought back memories of the bad, old days of the 1970s. In mid-2022, subway crime was up 58% year-over-year. "New York is suffering soaring crime because it has abruptly switched its justice system from enlightened prevention to gruesome mop-up," Gelinas wrote in Manhattan Institute's City Journal.

As New York and the nation coped with the pandemic, transit agencies found themselves adjusting to a new work-from-home trend, which has affected ridership levels and revenues. Off-peak commuting and cross-commuting dynamics are increasingly at play. Amid all this, calls continued for the MTA to improve itself from within.

"The pandemic is likely to have a long-term impact on the MTA, accelerating some trends, such as the rise of remote work, which were already underway before the pandemic," Tri-State's Blank told me. "The MTA is making some adjustments now, such as running more off-peak service and creating new discount fare packages, but these are largely just tinkering with the margins. They're good first steps, but they fall short of being transformational. The MTA needs to seriously rethink the commuter-rail operations and business model."

Foye left as MTA chairman when Cuomo tried to push him over to the interim presidency of the Empire State Development Corp. just three weeks before the governor himself resigned in disgrace in August 2021 in the face of sexual-harassment allegations. Foye rejected the Empire position.

Kathy Hochul succeeded Cuomo as governor and Janno Lieber became MTA chairman following a run as its chief development officer.

Lieber ran point on Silverstein Properties' initiative to rebuild the World Trade Center site after the Sept. 11 terrorist attacks and has brought a private-sector perspective to an agency that needed it.

Tribalism among the regional transportation agencies — the MTA, Port Authority of New York and New Jersey, and NJ Transit — remains a problem. In addition, quasi-public national carrier Amtrak has feuded with the MTA and its LIRR unit for years over track-sharing and union rules. Even within the MTA, in-house bickering between LIRR and Metro-North resulted in a more costly East Side Access project to funnel LIRR trains into Grand Central Terminal, several stories below street level. Cost estimates have risen from $3.5 billion in 2001 to $11.2 billion, plus $600 million in financing costs. The grand opening for the new station, Grand Central Madison, was scheduled for late in 2022.

Meanwhile, Hochul is moving ahead with a controversial Penn Station reconstruction project she inherited from Cuomo, which would circumvent the city's zoning process to seize and raze privately owned buildings and build a new set of skyscrapers.

"The bifurcated nature of the transit agencies will continue to be a problem for solving regional transportation, environmental and land use problems," Blank said. "We need to find a way to force the transit agencies to work together to implement 21st-century solutions, such as platform doors and Penn Station through-running."

Organizations, including the nonprofit ReThinkNYC, favor enabling the through-running of commuter rail at Penn Station. While Amtrak trains run through Penn Station along their Northeast Corridor routes, the station is now an end point for NJ Transit and LIRR trains. The MTA expects to complete its plan to funnel Metro-North trains into Penn Station — a project that would include four new stations in the East Bronx — by 2027.

Byford, speaking from London, cited the benefits of commuter through-running. He cited another megaproject. "[It] has certainly been a success in London with Thameslink being the most obvious example," he told me. "While many London-bound services terminate at the various termini that ring the capital, Thameslink has developed into a highly successful north/south through service that links two major airports, and that enables customers to traverse London without having to change."

Creative regional transportation options include further expanding ferry service across the boroughs. Queens Borough President Donovan Richards likes a concept the Port Authority has floated — forgive the pun — to add ferry service connecting LaGuardia Airport with Manhattan's East Side. The ferry idea is among about a dozen that Port Authority and state officials are weighing as an alternative to Cuomo's proposed AirTrain connector to Willets Point, Queens, which Hochul dropped shortly after taking office.

While skeptics point to low ferry ridership along existing routes, a boat connector is worth considering given that the region's three airports, LaGuardia, John F. Kennedy and Newark-Liberty, are so hard to access.

And let's take a cue from other countries. With gas prices skyrocketing and highways overcrowded, Deutsche Bahn, Germany's national train operator, launched a $10 monthly ticket for the summer months that covered the local and regional rail, though not high speed. Amtrak could do that and get people from New York to Boston, Philadelphia and Washington on the cheap. The Penn Station crowding would worsen, but you can't have everything. Implement similar discounts for subway and commuter rail as well.

Congestion pricing, meanwhile, is an X-factor for New York regional transit funding. A plan to charge vehicles entering Manhattan borough south of 60th Street is under federal environmental review at this writing, with implementation targeted for early 2023. The MTA projects that the plan could generate up to $15 billion annually through bonding. After some dead-on-arrival proposals going back nearly 40 years, New York state lawmakers approved congestion pricing as part of its budget package in April 2019. Whether it could roll out by the end of 2023 is an open question. Implementation variables include exemptions for certain groups.

"We are concerned that a lot of public backlash, especially from suburban folks and New Jersey elected officials, could persuade the TMRB [Traffic Mobility Review Board, which develops congestion pricing rules and rates] to include too many exemptions, which will increase the toll for everyone else," Blank said. New York Mayor Eric Adams, among others, has requested a series of exemptions.

Exemptions can get unwieldy, according to Mitchell Moss, director of New York University's Rudin Center for Transportation and Management. "You can't give spiritual healers a legitimate reason not to pay the tolls."

The Burg

Pennsylvania's capital city goes belly-up

In Harrisburg, the Pennsylvania capital that sits between state book-ends Philadelphia and Pittsburgh, a dark, foreboding incinerator four miles from downtown was ground zero in a disgraceful insolvency that featured municipal and banking corruption.

The city's story was tragic, though laced with absurdities.

A $25 million borrowing to retrofit the trash burner spiraled into $325 million of debt. The city couldn't get out of its own way: Its City Council filed for Chapter 9 bankruptcy protection in 2011 against the mayor's wishes, but a federal judge nullified the filing. As Harrisburg became part of the national discourse about municipal distress, conflicts were all over the lot: mayor vs. council, city vs. state, city vs. county, Main Street vs. Wall Street and black vs. white.

"For the longest time, I couldn't understand how a city could have been so financially raped," television journalist Chris Papst wrote in his book, "Capital Murder: An Investigative Reporter's Hunt for Answers in a Collapsing City."

"People were made massively wealthy issuing the bond deals that capsized Harrisburg," Papst wrote. "I watched as the protagonists who allowed it to happen hopped in their foreign sports sedans and fled town. They left behind a broke and broken city."

Players included a "mayor for life," Stephen Reed, who ultimately faced federal corruption charges; his acerbic successor, Linda Thompson; colorful attorney Mark Schwartz, who represented the City Council in its failed bankruptcy attempt; and the initial state-appointed receiver, David Unkovic, who was so stressed he said, "I wish my name was never out there," right before resigning. Unkovic, describing himself as being "in an untenable position in the political and ethical crosswinds," cited blowback from Gov. Tom Corbett's administration, lobbyists and lawmakers after he said major creditors should make concessions as part of Harrisburg's financial recovery. To some media folks, Unkovic's handwritten resignation note was fodder for armchair psychologists.

Unkovic's successor, retired Air Force general William Lynch, shepherded a financial recovery plan through after Corbett appointed him. The incinerator debt, in Lynch's own words, hung like "a dark cloud" over the city. Commonwealth Court judge Bonnie Brigance Leadbetter in September 2013 approved the plan, called Harrisburg Strong. Attaching the word "strong" was in vogue after Boston adopted it following the marathon bombing earlier that year.

The people part, said Lynch, was most difficult. "I had no idea when [Corbett] named me how complex this would be," he told me at the state finance building, across the street from the capitol. "Even for me, who's not a math person, the numbers part has not been the most difficult."

The approved plan erased about $600 million of overall crippling debt through measures that included the sale of the city incinerator to the Lancaster County Solid Waste Management Authority and a 40-year lease of parking assets. In addition, creditors took "haircuts," or less than full value of what they were owed. The plan also provided for a balanced city budget for four years and funding for infrastructure improvements, plus economic development incentives.

"Everybody needed something," said Steven Goldfield, a financial advisor to the reorganization plan and senior managing director at Public Resources Advisory Group outside Philadelphia. Major incinerator creditors included the media-unfriendly Assured Guaranty Municipal Corp. "AGM, for example, needed some good press. They needed a victory, and they knew the situation would not get any better, but could be worse," Goldfield said.

Locally, wariness abounded about anything Wall Street. One council member invoked a scene from the organized-crime movie "Goodfellas" while questioning the parking deal.

Reed, mayor from 1982 to 2010, engineered a buildout that included a downtown restaurant row, a Civil War museum and a minor-league baseball team that played on City Island, a recreational spot in the Susquehanna River.

While Reed basked for many years in the glow of city development, critics chafed over his heavy-handed ways. "His well-crafted media image directly opposed his executive style. He ran Harrisburg as if it were New York City or Chicago, though in public, he possessed an ability to turn a crowded room into an intimate setting," Papst said.

His apparent success over more than two decades made the city's debt crisis that much more compelling.

"Mayor Reed was one always thinking of ways to raise revenues for the City of Harrisburg. Eventually, some of those ideas turned into debt," said David Fiorenza, a prior associate professor of practice in the Villanova School of Business economics department, a visiting professor at Carnegie Mellon Heinz School of Public Policy and former municipal finance director for several Pennsylvania communities.

Before the city's implosion, Reed and his team drew praise as progressive revenue-and-budget innovators, Fiorenza said. "They would walk into the Pennsylvania state [Government Finance Officers Association] annual conference and heads would turn as we all knew the unique revenue enhancements and aggressive business tax collections they were doing for Harrisburg."

But after leaving office, Reed faced 200 criminal charges related to a Wild West museum that never materialized. Reed eventually pleaded guilty to 20 counts of theft for receiving stolen property in 2017. He received probation. Reed died in January 2020 after a long battle with prostate cancer.

"There were a number of projects going on in Central Pennsylvania that had no guarantees for the public but made profits for the people making the deals," said Joseph DiStefano, a veteran Philadelphia

Inquirer business columnist. "Philadelphia considered and dismissed the idea of a much larger incinerator at the time."

The crisis also offered multiple doses of Three Stooges–style slapstick to entertain media, both local and national.

In 2011, Thompson called four dissenting City Council members "unfit for public office" on the city's official website after repeated 4-to-3 votes to reject a state-sponsored reorganization plan. Meetings in the tiny first-floor council chamber at City Hall — as trucks from four television stations sat outside — were contentious. One council member, for example, scolded a colleague, telling her to "be an adult."

Thompson and City Comptroller Dan Miller didn't speak to each other, even as the city was spiraling into financial oblivion. Miller was a gay-and-lesbian advocate, while Thompson was deeply religious. According to the local Patriot-News, former Thompson media spokesman Chuck Ardo, who held the same position under ex-Gov. Ed Rendell for eight years, said the mayor regularly called Miller "that homosexual, evil little man" and wanted Ardo to tell the newspaper that Miller was an extortionist. Ardo resigned shortly thereafter.

In mid-2015, staff from the state attorney general's office raided Reed's ramshackle row-house apartment near the capitol and removed Wild West artifacts. They included wagon wheels, a life-sized sarcophagus or ancient stone coffin, a full suit of armor and a "vampire hunting kit." The Roxbury News, a local video website, filmed the event. "Saddle up, boys, giddy up," one agent said.

Thompson, who took a popemobile-style victory ride through downtown Harrisburg after her swearing in, was the city's first female mayor and first black mayor. She admirably overcame a teenage pregnancy to earn a degree from Howard University. "She's far better with numbers than I am," Lynch told me. "I have a lot of respect and a certain amount of affection for her. She inherited an awful situation, a disaster."

The debt crisis, for sure, wasn't her making. But she was a lightning rod for controversy. She blew kisses at people throwing snowballs at her office window, called residents of neighboring Perry County "scumbags" and dribbled a basketball over the dried blood of a murder victim during a press conference in the run-down Allison Hill neighborhood.

In August 2011, after yet another council 4-to-3 rejection of the state plan, a piss-and-vinegar Thompson held an impromptu press conference in her second-floor office. "The bond markets aren't willing to touch this city with all the chaos and all the dysfunction that's going on," she said. I was one of the last of the media to get inside before she told her aide: "Lock the door, lock the door." A bowl of small candies sat in the middle of the table. No one dared touch any. When I left after the press conference, some locked-out media were in the corridor. "What the hell? What just happened?" Papst said. "She locked us out; I can't believe it."

In my sit-down with Thompson late in 2013 shortly before she left office, she smiled when I asked her about critics who called her ill-tempered, divisive, paranoid and overly religious. "I was portrayed as this crazy black female who had everyone praying in her office," she said. "It was like Jesus being led to the slaughterhouse." The candy bowl was still there, and I took a piece on the way out.

Harrisburg was one of several municipal distress stories in the early 2010s as the nation struggled to come out of a severe recession. The problems of Detroit and Puerto Rico eventually became well-headlined bankruptcy cases. Three California communities filed for Chapter 9 insolvency. So did Jefferson County, Alabama. Ditto for 18,000-population Rhode Island city Central Falls, which consumed only one square mile but cited an $80 million unfunded pension liability.

In Pennsylvania, which former national Democratic Party consultant James Carville once described as "Philadelphia, Pittsburgh and a lot of Alabama in-between," cities struggled to get funding from state lawmakers. "It's every single municipality," Miller said. "The legislature just doesn't want to do anything for the urban areas. We can't expand revenue and we can't control costs. We have the unions and arbitration laws working against us, so we're stuck in this tight squeeze."

Racial overtones provided another backdrop to Harrisburg. After Pennsylvania's legislature quickly passed a law effectively prohibiting the city from filing for bankruptcy under Chapter 9, one council member said Republican suburban lawmakers put a bull's-eye on Harrisburg because its mayor and five of its seven councilors — all Democrats –— were African-American.

The plights of Harrisburg and Central Falls drew parallel discussions. Law firms and bond-rating agencies held web seminars. I did a feature-length piece packaging the two cities within a wider municipal-distress context. When I talked by phone from Harrisburg with Central Falls receiver Bob Flanders, he was curious about what was going on in Pennsylvania. Likewise, during a City Council meeting recess in Harrisburg, one local public agency head asked me: "What's going on in Central Falls?" It was a weird form of keeping up with the Joneses.

Much of Harrisburg's backstory flew under the national-media radar. "Some large media, such as Reuters and the Bond Buyer, continued to follow the story, but most didn't," Papst wrote.

Covering municipal distress was great for my own exposure. I did several media interviews on the topic, including a 30-second spot with Papst in 2015 as part of a six-minute segment on "Full Measure," a nationally syndicated documentary show hosted by former CBS News White House correspondent Sharyl Attkisson. "Debt Danger" was the headline of the segment. I called the Harrisburg crisis "a day of reckoning" for Wall Street. Well, maybe not, but it made a good sound bite. Philadelphia public radio also interviewed me about municipal distress in general, while CBS Radio had me on the air to discuss why Connecticut capital Hartford was a dumpster fire.

In her reelection bid in 2013, Thompson said of Democratic primary challenger Eric Papenfuse: "All he's ever done is own a bookstore." Sensing fun with that one, I called Papenfuse, owner of the popular local Midtown Scholar Bookstore, which hosted several public sessions about the debt crisis. His reply: "I would like to think that the mayor would be supportive of a local business that is successful and promotes literacy." Papenfuse won that primary and was mayor from 2014 to 2021. "I've invested in a bookstore, I own my own home and have three young children, all born in Harrisburg," he said. "I'm completely invested in this city, and it's been frustrating to witness the political in-fighting from the sidelines and not get involved. If you lived in Harrisburg, you'd feel compelled to get involved too."

Mark Schwartz, a Bryn Mawr, Pennsylvania, solo practitioner, represented the City Council when it filed for bankruptcy against the wishes of Thompson and Dauphin County, while Corbett and other top state officials feared that Pennsylvania's other distressed communities would file similarly. "Contagion" became a municipal-distress buzzword.

Schwartz, known for his whistleblowing and civil-rights advocacy, said Prudential-Bache Securities fired him in 1989 after he complained about threats being made to investment bankers who did not make campaign contributions to help win bond business. Schwartz, who once played author Truman Capote in an off-Broadway play, made good copy. He could say anything. My favorite quote from him was about Pennsylvania's Department of Community and Economic Development, which coordinated the state's financial recovery program for distressed communities: "Send them a corpse and they'll rubber-stamp it."

Schwartz likened the incinerator bond financial deals to Ponzi schemes. "The people who committed the financial equivalent of murder got away with it," he once told me. He counseled Reed briefly after his indictment. "Mayor Reed hardly put a gun to the head of bond counsel and other bond issue participants who abdicated their legal responsibilities in favor of reaping millions of dollars in fees. These are the true villains of Harrisburg."

Harrisburg, sadly, is no corruption outlier in Pennsylvania. The most notorious case was that of State Treasurer Budd Dwyer, convicted of bribery and facing up to 55 years in prison. Dwyer, one day before his scheduled sentencing in January 1987, pulled out a .357 Magnum at a news conference and shot himself in the mouth. The public suicide caught viewers off guard and triggered soul-searching in newsrooms throughout the country over coverage of such events. Some TV stations aired the entire footage. Others cut off the tape as Dwyer pointed the gun toward his face. Editor & Publisher magazine, considered a journalistic bible at the time, ran a lengthy spread that weighed best practices in these situations.

I saw the full footage years later and wished I hadn't.

Subsequent state treasurers Barbara Hafer and Rob McCord were also ensnared in corruption scandals. More recently, Kathleen Kane, who as state attorney general announced the indictments against Reed and pontificated at that press conference about municipal corruption, was later convicted of leaking details about a grand jury investigation in Philadelphia and lying about it.

Before her problems surfaced, Pennsylvania Democrats touted Kane as the "it girl." In 2012 she earned more votes than President Obama in becoming the state's first female attorney general. She resigned after her 2016 conviction. "Look back a few years, when Kane's tenure as attorney general was still in its honeymoon phase. The media was enthralled by her rags-to-riches personal story, and certain corners of the political establishment were positively giddy over her seemingly limitless potential," David Gambacorta wrote in Philadelphia magazine. Kane served an eight-month prison sentence and was disbarred.

In 2022 Kane was back in the news, violating her probation with her arrest for drunk driving. A judge ordered her to a residential alcohol treatment center.

In Allentown, former Mayor Ed Pawlowski received a 15-year sentence for his conviction in a pay-to-play corruption scheme from 2012 to 2015 regarding the issuance of city contracts and other business. Under Pawlowski's watch, 120,000-population Allentown launched several economic development initiatives, two of which, considered together, won the Bond Buyer's Northeast Deal of the Year award in 2013.

We frequently joked about a "Deal of the Year jinx." Detroit, under then-Mayor Kwame Kilpatrick, received the newspaper's national award in 2005 for a $1.4 billion borrowing deal called pension obligation certificates of participation, designed to eliminate the city's unfunded pension liabilities. Lawyers during Detroit's bankruptcy proceedings called the deal "a sham." Kilpatrick served more than seven years of a 28-year prison sentence for corruption crimes before President Trump, shortly before leaving office, commuted his sentence. Richard Ravitch, one of New York City's top power brokers for over half a century, needled me often about that Detroit award.

Scranton Mayor Bill Courtright in October 2020 received seven years for criminal conspiracy, bribery and extortion. The FBI's undercover investigation revealed him accepting cash payments from vendors doing business with the city. Under Courtright's successor, Paige Cognetti, the city in 2022 exited Pennsylvania's program for distressed communities, known commonly as Act 47. Harrisburg is still in it. Former Reading Mayor Vaughn Spencer in 2019 received an eight-year sentence after a jury convicted him of bribery, wire fraud and conspiracy.

"Mayors who are elected would like to thank their donors in the form of contracts," Fiorenza said. "This is not just for contractors, but professional services such as bond counsel, investment firms and insurance brokers.

"The common thread is there are not enough checks and balances at the county or state level [on] those in power, such as mayors, borough managers and township managers. I knew three suburban municipal managers, on a professional level, who started to overstep their boundaries with personal expenses and not adhering to their contract with the elected officials."

Fiorenza favors requiring municipal governments to change their independent auditors every four to six years instead of reappointing the same firm for a lifetime. Compounding the oversight problem is that the state, in an effort to save money, downsized such departments as the auditor general's office.

"In my three-plus decades of municipal service, I have seen the state audits of pension and even liquid fuels [tax] audits behind, in some cases, by several years," Fiorenza said. "This lapse in time is another indication of how long it can take to reveal problems in a Pennsylvania city or municipality."

Detroit exited Chapter 9 late in 2014 after only 16 months in bankruptcy court. Its roughly $18 billion of debt paled in comparison with Puerto Rico's $70 billion. The island territory, which filed under a Chapter 9 equivalent, exited bankruptcy early in 2022.

DiStefano praised the work of David Skeel, the University of Pennsylvania law professor and bankruptcy expert who chaired the federal oversight board that controlled Puerto Rico's finances. "Skeel took a lot of abuse from both sides, but he was very impressive," he said. Puerto Rico exited bankruptcy early in 2022.

Harrisburg's finances have somewhat stabilized over the years, and the state enhanced the city's taxing authority to help on the revenue side. Still, the poverty rate is roughly 30% and as a state capital, much of Harrisburg's revenue is tax-exempt. At City Hall, longtime council member Wanda Williams succeeded Papenfuse as mayor in January 2022. Williams knows all too well the city's struggles, financially and otherwise. Stray gunfire killed one of her granddaughters when the girl was an innocent bystander. "She will need to work collaboratively with City Council, as well as with county and state officials, some of whom can be, well, difficult," the Patriot-News editorialized.

The takeaway from Harrisburg, Fiorenza said, is that continually poor decision-making can happen in any municipality.

"External and state audits do not catch everything, so having citizen advisory groups and panels can keep the politicians focused on what is really fiscally sound in the long-term," he said. "Ethical public officials' responsibility needs to be emphasized at the undergraduate and graduate levels of our higher education institutions. Each student should be required to participate in a course related to ethics. There will be some point at which most people will have some involvement with the public sector, not directly but could be indirectly."

Background checks that precede hiring municipal employees or electing officials will often show no illegal infractions, he added. "Most of these issues occur after the person is in office and the power and greed overwhelm their good fiscal intentions."

An intriguing trial

*Muni bond bankers face federal
bid-rigging charges*

One of my most intriguing assignments was the 2012 municipal bond bid-rigging trial in New York, *US v. Carollo, Grimm and Goldberg.* It revolved around federal allegations that Dominick Carollo, Peter Grimm and Steven Goldberg — former bankers at GE Funding Capital Market Services — rigged the bidding process for municipal bond contracts, costing state and local issuers millions of dollars.

The scheme, which occurred from 1999 to 2006, included accusations of providing "last looks" about competitors' bids, intentionally submitting losing bids and arranging for kickbacks through back-end swap agreements.

I didn't tell anyone at the time, but it was my first court case in more than 40 years and my first criminal trial ever. And I've covered everything from presidential press conferences to pro hockey. While I had little experience covering the courts, I didn't need any. My approach was simple: Research the hell out of the case, then go there, paint a vivid picture and capture the color.

If you're not a bond expert, you're in good company because neither was most of the jury in the beginning. A municipal bond sounds like something abstract and complex, but think of it this way — a bond is debt. Remember that and you'll be fine. States, counties and cities — often called issuers — borrow from Wall Street banks to build and fix roads, bridges and schools and for other projects.

So, what is bid rigging, anyway?

According to the federal government, bid rigging can take many forms. One common method is when competitors agree in advance which firm will win the bid.

Municipal officials often hire brokers, or middleman firms, to arrange an auction and invite banks to compete for a community's business and bid on interest rates. Under a competitive system, the highest interest rate wins the bid. It's supposed to be fair-market, but according to prosecutors, our three bankers gamed the system through phony actions that essentially divided up the winnings.

How did they do that?

Instead of a competitive auction in which no one knew of anyone else's interest rates, the bankers allegedly prearranged a "winner" by revealing the bids to the other competitors. That enabled the "winning" bank to lower its offer to an interest rate just high enough to beat out its so-called competitors. In industry parlance, that's called a "last look." It's kind of like point-shaving in basketball, in which players on a team collude to take a bribe not necessarily to lose a game, but to win by fewer points than expected so that bookies can make money.

In return the winning bank would pay the broker through kickbacks disguised as fees for unrelated transactions.

The bottom line is that these apparent "nickel-and-diming" measures by Wall Street cost states, cities and towns millions of dollars for about a decade while a handful of characters profited at their expense.

The case also reflected corruption within the securities industry, both in municipal bonds and elsewhere. During a podcast with Philadelphia-area whistleblower attorney Mark Schwartz, I brought up the need to overhaul the regulation of munis, and he recalled his early days working for a Pittsburgh law firm.

"I once said to the head of the firm, and the firm did exclusively municipal bond work ... why doesn't a Ralph Nader look into this? And he said, 'Shhhhh, be quiet,'" Schwartz said. "I've never understood why municipal bonds aren't subject to registration like any other form of security. It would just alleviate a lot of problems."

Schwartz sees regulators as clueless. He cited one of his whistle-blowing cases in particular.

"I ended up with a guy at the SEC [Securities and Exchange Commission] in Philadelphia — makes quarter of a million dollars. He didn't know what insider trading was, making a quarter of a million dollars a year. I mean, I used to think that regulators wanted to go through the revolving door to get into Wall Street. Now I think that they're fat, dumb and happy and just want to stay in their jobs and not perform."

This trial took place in the throes of the Great Recession and with negative attitudes about Wall Street. So here came your prototypical Wall Street people accused of stealing taxpayer money.

Municipal bond scandals are nothing new.

A former broker-dealer firm named Matthews & Wright was forced out of the municipal market in the 1980s after underwriting dozens of questionable bond deals, notably one for East St. Louis, Illinois, an impoverished city across the Mississippi River from St. Louis. "There was no Matthews and there was no Wright," a former bond lawyer said. "They took a couple of waspy names out of the phone book."

Bid rigging, though, is extremely difficult to prove, and one of the more fascinating aspects of the case was how the prosecutors built their case on tapes.

The tapes were more than just tools for the prosecution and debate points for the defense. They brought a whole new dynamic to the trial: tapes, tapes and more tapes.

"The tapes, of course, were very crucial because nothing is stronger than convicting someone of the words out of their own mouth," St. John's University law professor Anthony Sabino told me. "And in this instance, because of the sophistication of the parties involved and the financial transactions, they worked at institutions where the tape recording of conversations was done on a constant basis.

"So, there were tapes. They were retained for business reasons so they were available, and the government was able to prove its case by putting all those tapes out there, and again, I have to commend the jury because they spent many days listening to these tapes."

The trial was in the 23rd floor at the federal courthouse just off Foley Square in Lower Manhattan. The room resembled what you see in "Law & Order" episodes. Many of the people on opening day were lawyers studying the case.

Only journalists embedded in the courthouse — working out of an office there, in other words — could carry electronic equipment inside. Due to post-9/11 precautions, I had to check in my laptop, cellphone and portable recorder after entering the Worth Street side entrance. I found myself calling sources and filing bulletins to make our deadline while sitting outside on the courthouse steps.

At one point I described the proceedings as "equal parts titillating and tedious."

The main characters, a motley crew of sorts, included presiding Judge Harold Baer, age 79 at the time and limping with a cane. When you rode the elevator with him, you realized how much pain he was in. Baer was best known for his liberal interpretations on civil liberties cases in the 1990s that upset President Bill Clinton and New York Mayor Rudy Giuliani.

Baer ran the courtroom with a pleasant sarcasm and bantered well with prosecutors, the defense attorneys and the jury. He was sympathetic that many jurors, including people among the working poor, might not understand the nuances of the municipal bond industry.

Baer died two years after the trial.

In his opening remarks, he said he didn't expect much media coverage. But I was there almost daily for the Bond Buyer, and investigative reporter Matt Taibbi wrote two colorful pieces about the trial in Rolling Stone magazine. Coverage from other media was sporadic. It took little time for people to know who I was. In fact, Walter Timpone, the lawyer for defendant Carollo and later a New Jersey Supreme Court associate justice, came up to me in the middle of the week, smiled and said, "Is it Friday yet?" Clearly Timpone and the other *dramatis personae* knew they were in for a grinding three weeks.

Running point for the prosecution was Wendy Waszmer, diminutive and tenacious. She reminded me of a younger version of Linda Hunt's character Hetty Lange on the CBS-TV show "NCIS: Los Angeles." Taibbi called her "the feisty federal prosecutor with straight brown hair and an elfin build."

The most vocal of the defense counsel was John Siffert, who represented Goldberg. Siffert, a founding partner in New York's Lankler Siffert & Wohl, loved the big stage, enjoyed the sound of his own voice and bantered well with Baer. Taibbi found nothing likeable about Siffert, but I enjoyed him. He had a touch of Eddie Haskell, the smart-aleck teen character Ken Osmond played on the old TV show "Leave It to Beaver."

Siffert's official position on the case was "no comment," but he often provided me insights on background. He also asked me to email him posted versions of my stories so he could show them to his elderly father. Siffert loved the publicity.

I respected the defendants' wishes to not talk about the case. Yet I was able to make off-the-record small talk with two of them. During breaks in the proceedings, Goldberg and I would peer out the 23rd-floor windows and, together, guessed which streets were running north-south: Mott Street … Mulberry … The Bowery. I shared elevator rides with Carollo and his family, and we talked about the better food options in the eighth-floor cafeteria after a new vendor took over.

Witnesses included British-born Adrian Scott-Jones, a government witness and a recovering alcoholic who recalled a certain meeting between bankers because "the sake was exceptionally good." Siffert, bolstered by inconsistencies in Scott-Jones' testimony that emerged on tape, smelled blood in the water on cross-examination. "You can savor the sake in your mouth as you sit here today, right?"

Forgive the expression, but Baer kept a dry wit about it all. During one exchange about meetings in Italian and Asian restaurants, he said, "I think the jury can tell the difference between lasagna and sake."

Scott-Jones did not return that afternoon, and at his sentencing months later, his attorney, Adria Perez, admitted he tried to hurt himself. She said: "He was alone up on the stand, and his feeling was, 'Where can I find the nearest hardware store to buy a knife?'" Perez also said her client, with a history of depression and anxiety, "had an incident with a bottle of Scotch and some Tylenol and a second incident with a chainsaw." Perez criticized Justice Department prosecutors for not objecting strongly enough to Siffert's questioning methods.

Among the government witnesses were people who got caught and flipped. One of them told of a federal raid on his California office. He wasn't there. He said he read about it after the fact in the Bond Buyer.

I always took pride in journalistic neutrality and figured if both sides liked or disliked your coverage equally, then you were doing your job well. While I had a rapport with members of the defense teams, people from the U.S. Securities and Exchange Commission also approached me saying they enjoyed our coverage.

The trial ran for three weeks. Deliberations lasted four days. The atmosphere got giddy while jurors were out, as though to break the mood. On one day, antagonists Waszmer and Siffert sat in the empty jury box, laughing and yucking it up while poring over a newspaper. I wrote about the levity in one of my downtime pieces, and it pissed off Siffert. "Hey Paul, what's said on this side, stays on this side," he said, also loud enough for the whole courtroom to hear.

The specter of a divided jury loomed at one point, when jurors asked Baer how they should mark a jury questionnaire box if they could not reach a unanimous decision on "a particular count for a specific defendant." Baer told the jurors to keep on talking.

"Continue deliberating," he said.

They did, and the very next day — the afternoon of Friday, May 11, 2012 — Baer's clerk, a man named Dennis, walked in waving a sheet of paper. "We have a verdict," he shouted. The courtroom became eerily silent.

The jury returned. Guilty on all nine counts. Four on Goldberg, three on Grimm and two on Carollo. As sobs from family members rippled throughout the courtroom, the federal team formed a human phalanx around tiny prosecutor Waszmer and escorted her out of the courtroom.

Defense attorneys, even the vocal Siffert, sat stunned. He had little to offer when I approached him, just saying the defense attorneys would file post-trial motions.

The quality of legal work on both sides of the aisle impressed Lathrop Nelson, a partner with Montgomery McCracken Walker & Rhoads.

"In reading about the trial and following the trial, which I did, I was impressed with the lawyering on all sides. I think the individual defendants were very well represented and the government put on a good case," Nelson told me on a special-edition Bond Buyer podcast we recorded at his Philadelphia office.

Internally, the handful of us involved with the podcast, including the editor-in-chief, kept higher-ups out of the loop because we didn't want their meddling. Because the company's open-plan office setup offered little privacy, we spoke in code. I named the project "Eagle II," the eagle referring to the nickname of my favorite hockey team, Boston College. We spoke internally about promoting the podcast extensively, including to college law schools, but in the end, the company, to no surprise, ran it as just another podcast while slapping the words "special edition" on it. SourceMedia/Arizent was always loath to publicize the work of its individual journalists.

Nelson was tangentially involved in the appeal. His firm had represented a third party and filed a motion for protective order during the appeal of that case, but was otherwise not involved.

Defense lawyers, meanwhile, had an ace in their hands — the statute of limitations. It forbids prosecutors from charging someone with a crime committed more than a certain number of years ago. Its purpose is to ensure that convictions occur only upon evidence that has not deteriorated over time.

After the trial, the defense team set out for an appeal, confident they would win on that basis, on the statute of limitations.

A few months after the verdict, Carollo counsel Timpone held a reporter's gaggle outside the courtroom during sentencing for cooperating witnesses.

When I asked him how confident he was about the appeal, he said, "Very, actually."

Appeals rested primarily on the argument that the government did not move quickly enough to indict them after the alleged fraud and on whether the statute of limitations in these crimes were ongoing or had expired. U.S. Department of Justice lawyers argued that the fraudulently awarded contracts included interest payments that harmed the public well after the turn-of-the-millennium bidding, invalidating the statute of limitations defense.

In November 2013, a three-judge Second Circuit appeals court, in a 2-1 vote, overturned the guilty verdicts and ordered the release of Grimm, Carollo and Goldberg before Thanksgiving.

"When the government brought the case, they were beyond the standard five-year statute of limitations for any of the actual bid-rigging that was alleged to have occurred, and what they claimed was that with each provider's payment — of a payment pursuant to the investment contract — that constituted an act in furtherance of the conspiracy," Nelson said.

These contracts were 20 to 25 years in length.

The appeals court cited a case from the First Circuit, when Stephen Bryor — later a Supreme Court justice — said, as Nelson put it, "Where a series of payments are lengthy, indefinite, ordinary, typically non-criminal and unilateral in scope, and there's no threat of any continuing conduct, that those payments, even though they are the beneficiaries of the fraudulent conduct, those don't consist of overt acts or furtherance of the conspiracy."

The following August, a split Second Circuit voted 8-4 to not hear the case *en banc*, or before a full panel of judges.

The defendants went free and left us wondering if the government, despite its white-collar sweep of muni bond bankers, dropped the ball.

Or are these cases just hard to prosecute, say, as opposed to drug cases, because of their degrees of difficulty?

"I would say both," Sabino said. "On one hand, white-collar cases are difficult to prosecute. You're dealing with a highly educated, more sophisticated type of putative felon, and for that reason they're a little bit better at covering their tracks. Indeed, particular to this case was the fact that it was a conspiracy case. Conspiracies are the most difficult to prove of any criminal matter.

"But on the other hand, I think an equal part was the government was a little bit asleep on the switch."

The government could have advanced the case by 12 months and filed just under the deadline. "How these very capable prosecutors here in New York missed that makes one wonder," Sabino said.

In many other related cases, the government took plea bargains. Renowned federal judge Kimba Wood — whom Bill Clinton once nominated for U.S. attorney general, but then withdrew the offer because of a nannygate fiasco — presided over some of them.

Wood was a marquee name in legal circles for her personal and professional history, but she underwhelmed me. She was harsh on Michael Milken in 1990, sentencing the junk-bond king to 10 years in prison, although the sentence was reduced to two years' imprisonment and three years' probation. However, she was soft, even fawning, on the bid riggers who pleaded out. And many of them were broke, limiting the fines she could impose.

According to Sabino, prosecutors could have been a little more savvy.

"One thing I've learned about defending white-collar criminals and going after them in a prior career is that bad people tend to be repeat offenders. They'll do the bad thing yet again. ... Let's keep an eye on these guys, and let's see if they do it again."

The point of the appeal is not to protect the bad guys, but rather the rest of us.

"If we don't strictly enforce statutes of limitations — the amount of time in which the government can prosecute any one of us — then that means for the rest of our lives, for wrongs committed or wrongs never committed or wrongs thought to be committed, the government can come after us at any time of their choosing, and that's not simply fair under our system of justice," Sabino said.

Even if you don't understand bonds, or bid rigging, you certainly understand corruption. You understand the government dropping the ball. You understand how people play fast and loose with our lives, our data, our personal information. Today big-data companies track every move we make online. We have red-light cameras and "vaccine passports," thanks to COVID-19.

"While I would say as a personal matter, I'm somewhat disappointed with the end result here. The bottom line is that as an American, I'm very satisfied because this is what's required under our system of justice," Sabino said. "If the government cannot bring a prosecution within the requisite period of time, then they've lost that opportunity."

Swing and a miss

Curt Schilling's video-game company strikes out in Rhode Island

Mix a wobbly economy, an infatuation with celebrities and some dark political intrigue, and what do you get?

The 38 Studios bond financing scandal in Rhode Island.

In 2010 the state issued a $75 million loan that then-Gov. Don Carcieri brokered to entice former baseball pitcher Curt Schilling to move his video-game company, 38 Studios, to capital city Providence from Maynard, Massachusetts. Rhode Island, its economy reeling at the time, envisioned an economic development buildout through tech. Schilling wore jersey number 38 while playing. His company's original name was Green Monster Games, in honor of the iconic left-field wall at Boston's Fenway Park.

The company went belly-up two years later. Rhode Island had to cover the debt because it issued a "moral obligation" guarantee with the bonds it sold to finance the undertaking.

"38 Studios was a story that had everything: celebrity, money, politics, backroom deals and a narrative arc worthy of a novel," said Ted Nesi, political and business editor for WPRI-TV in Providence and author of a popular weekly blog "Nesi's Notes."

"For local media, there were a lot of reasons we spent so much time on it — the amount of money involved was significant, Curt Schilling was a household name and it raised serious questions about the competence of Rhode Island officials," Nesi said. "Those factors were also there for the national media, but I think for outsiders there was also an element of seeing Rhode Island as a uniquely quirky place where this kind of thing could happen."

Schilling, who helped the Boston Red Sox win their first two World Series championships since 1918 and also pitched in the Fall Classic for the Philadelphia Phillies and Arizona Diamondbacks, was a video-game enthusiast who had hoped to cash in on his celebrity.

His winning performance in Game 6 of the 2004 American League Championship Series, pitching after foot surgery and sporting a bloody sock, was the stuff of legends. "Schilling's performance tonight will long live in New England baseball lore," Fox Sports broadcaster Tim McCarver said as Schilling left the game after the seventh inning, having yielded only one run and four hits. The Red Sox defeated the New York Yankees 4-2 that evening and 10-3 one night later to complete baseball's only comeback from a 3-0 series deficit. They captured their first World Series championship since 1918 one week later.

Schilling was a ballsy sort who talked a good game and often backed it up. When the Red Sox signed him for 2004, Schilling immediately seized the moment. As the season began, he appeared on a Boston television ad, hitching a ride into town and telling the driver, "I'm here to end an 86-year hex."

The Yankees lorded over the Red Sox for most of a century. Boston was coming off an especially torturous seven-game loss in 2003 to its hated rivals in the American League Championship Series. As the Red Sox-Yankees playoff rematch loomed, Schilling shot off his mouth again. "I'm not sure I can think of any scenario more enjoyable than making 55,000 people from New York shut up," he told reporters. Asked about the "mystique and aura" of the Yankees, he suggested Mystique and Aura were a pair of exotic dancers.

Schilling retired after the 2007 World Series, during which he won another game as the Red Sox swept the Colorado Rockies.

Still, not even his celebrity could get him funding from Massachusetts officials. For them the sketchy nature of the video-game industry was a giant red flag. Nonetheless, Rhode Island, staring at one of the nation's highest unemployment rates, approved a $75 million economic development deal for Schilling to move his company to the Ocean State and complete the multiplayer online video game "Project Copernicus."

But the video game company belonging to the man with the bloody sock was a bloody mess. 38 Studios collapsed in 2012, missing a loan payment and then filing for Chapter 7 liquidation and leaving Rhode Island on the hook for the loan. Schilling laid off his entire staff of roughly 400 people in Providence and Timonium, Maryland.

"I wish I weren't standing here right now," Lincoln Chafee, governor at the time, said at a related news conference in May.

Fast forward to June 2014, when state lawmakers were investigating that bond deal.

I interviewed two of them — Democrat Karen MacBeth of Cumberland and Republican Michael Chippendale from Foster — about threatening letters they received, warning them to "stop poking around." We met in a cluttered basement office at the State Capitol, which contrasted with the grandeur of the building's exterior that overlooked downtown Providence from Smith Hill. My radar for political bullshit is sharp, but the look on MacBeth's face was real. "If anything happens to me …" she said as she unlocked the door, sentence tailing off.

Rhode Island politics were in turmoil in 2014. Gordon Fox had resigned earlier that year as House speaker and later served three years in a federal prison after pleading guilty to wire fraud, bribery and filing a false tax return. All the while the state rehired its financial advisor, First Southwest, even though it was suing that bank and others looking to reclaim lost money from 38 Studios.

"This falls into the 'only in Rhode Island' type of thing," Chippendale said.

MacBeth and Chippendale received their threatening letters in late April after inquiring to state officials about an unfinished forensic audit Chafee had ordered from the state's Economic Development Commission.

The threats deepened their resolve, they said in their joint interview with me. "Now it's personal," said Chippendale, who received his letter first. At the time he was one of six Republicans in the 75-seat House. "I'm a Republican. There are fewer of us here, and the mail is easier to sort," he said, grinning.

According to Chippendale, the letter said: "You have a beautiful family. For their sake, stop poking around." MacBeth wouldn't specify the wording in the letter she received but said it was similar. "They used the same font," she said.

They said few inside the capitol knew they were "poking around." Chippendale said he spent $2,000 for a new security system on his home. "I know how to rekey my door lock now," MacBeth said.

MacBeth, a fascinating study, hardly fit the municipal bond gadfly prototype. She was the principal of Harris Elementary School in Woonsocket and a mother, with three children. MacBeth entered politics as a children's advocate. After a stint on the Cumberland school committee, she won an open-seat election for state representative.

"When I first got to the House, I didn't even know what a speaker was," she said in one of my all-time favorite quotes. But over time she ascended to an oversight committee chairmanship, and into the 38 Studios cauldron.

MacBeth voted for the bill in 2010 but says she since sharpened her radar. She said the deal didn't pass the stink test. "I was told this was a jobs-creation bill, and I was lied to," she said.

MacBeth switched to the Republican Party in 2016.

"With Karen, it's all about right and wrong," said Michael Riley, co-founder of Narragansett, Rhode Island, investment firm Coastal Management Group LLC and a former Republican candidate for Congress. Riley asked the FBI's Boston office to investigate a sale of $1.2 million in 38 Studios bonds one day before Schilling laid off his employees by email.

Riley said the unidentified trader made a profit of almost $200,000. "This is known as insider trading. It stinks," he told me in a hotel lobby at India Point along the Providence waterfront. "I wasn't really looking for 38 Studios — there had been only 42 trades in three years — but then this one really jumped out at me."

The fiasco embarrassed Rhode Island and saddled the state with so-called moral obligation debt.

State officials heard the footsteps of bond-rating agencies, who threatened the state with downgrades if it didn't make annual payments on the bonds. The rating agencies, in effect, equated Rhode Island's moral obligation — a moral commitment to avoid defaulting on payments — to the more binding general obligation.

"How in the world could they have given away the store and made the majority of those bonds available to a company that was never in the black and was never properly vetted?" said Anthony Figliola, a vice president at Empire Government Strategies, a Uniondale, New York, consulting firm and a 2022 congressional candidate.

Fallout from 38 Studios also hovered over two stadium proposals for the Boston Red Sox minor-league affiliate in Pawtucket, where future major league stars Wade Boggs and Jim Rice once played. The first plan, on vacated Interstate 195 land near downtown Providence, fizzled as did one for Pawtucket itself. That prompted the team to announce in 2018 that it would leave for Worcester, Massachusetts, where they began play in 2021 at the new Polar Park in that city's Canal District.

Typically, finger-pointing in Rhode Island followed the loss of the team. Cranston Mayor Allan Fung, the Republican candidate for governor in 2018 and a congressional hopeful in 2022, blamed "a dysfunctional relationship" between Gov. Gina Raimondo, House Speaker Nicholas Mattiello and Senate President Dominick Ruggerio. Mattiello blamed team owners. Ruggerio, in turn, lambasted Mattiello for changing a Senate-approved bond bill intended to keep the team in Pawtucket.

Pawtucket became a battleground with more mingling of sports, economic development and taxpayer dollars — and the ghost of 38 Studios cast a huge shadow. Proponents touted the economic-development needs for a 76,000- population city, while opponents, an odd mix of conservatives and progressives, were wary of using state bonding to benefit a private entity.

Both sides played the 38 Studios card. Supporters said the deal was much different, while opponents called it a fiasco revisited.

"One thing we should have learned from 38 Studios is that taxpayers should have some say when borrowing is issued in the name of economic development," Republican national committeeman Steve Frias said. "Economists for decades have said that sports stadiums do not deliver on jobs and economic development. They rely on overly rosy projections, and the taxpayers wind up paying the bill.

"You have to question whether bond buyers will buy these bonds at 5% after the experience Rhode Island had with 38 Studios," Frias added. "There's also a fear of inside politics."

Skittishness resonated with voters and some public officials. "People in Rhode Island have such a sour taste from 38 Studios," Raimondo told me late in 2015. "It was a terrible deal from day one, but we can't let that paralyze us while we're trying to rebound from a weak economy."

According to WPRI's Nesi, the Pawtucket baseball stadium brouhaha represented a prime example of 38 Studios backlash.

"A lot has changed since the pandemic. Because it has overshadowed everything, we don't really know what 'normal' political debates will look like once it's over," he said. "But certainly prior to the pandemic, a quick way to tarnish any proposal was to call it 'another 38 Studios.'

"A prime example of that was the [stadium] debate. There were a lot of arguments made against the plan by opponents, but some of them pointed to questions about bond repayments and who would be on the hook for what — those debates might have seemed esoteric if taxpayers hadn't gone through the 38 Studios experience."

A planned $124 million soccer stadium and related economic development to replace the departed PawSox is in the works. In July 2022 the Rhode Island Commerce Corp. — the Economic Development Commission rebranded — approved the controversial proposal by a 6-to-5 margin, with Gov. Dan McKee casting the tiebreaking vote.

Rhode Island for years has been trying to beat back its reputation for corruption. Following up after New York Gov. Andrew Cuomo resigned in disgrace in August 2021, the Washington Post named Rhode Island one of the six most corrupt states.

Convicted felon Vincent "Buddy" Cianci served two terms as Providence mayor and even hosted his own radio talk show. An off-Broadway musical chronicled his life. Providence was also New England's organized crime headquarters for years, with Raymond Patriarca running the operation out of the Federal Hill neighborhood in an office adjacent to some popular restaurants.

Fox wound up in the slammer for taking a $52,000 bribe to fix a liquor license. He also spent $108,000 of campaign funds on himself and filed a false tax return. Charles Moreau, the mayor of bankrupt Central Falls, pleaded guilty in 2012 to accepting bribes in exchange for awarding a contract to board up foreclosed homes within the city. And in 2017 former House finance committee Chairman Ray Gallison served more than four years in federal prison for stealing from a dead man's estate and a special needs trust.

The list goes on and on.

"Why go to Rhode Island? They're all corrupt there," one bond analyst said to me before a planned visit. I relayed that to Raimondo in one of my sit-downs with the governor. Normally glib and media friendly, she was momentarily stunned — she probably counted to 10 in her head before giving a boilerplate response.

Raimondo, who made national headlines as state treasurer when she championed a law overhauling the state's public-pension system, became President Biden's commerce secretary early in 2021.

Rhode Island has much going for it. Its beaches are first-rate and Ivy League Brown University, on College Hill east of downtown, is a fun place to kick around. Just drive uphill and spare yourself the grueling walk. Rhode Island School of Design boasts a terrific museum at the foot of College Hill, and the city's WaterFire exhibit along the Providence River is a major tourist attraction. And Providence College, long steeped in basketball tradition, is also home to the 2015 national men's hockey champion Friars.

Raimondo's former press secretary, Marie Aberger, used to implore me to dine at quintessentially Rhode Island eateries. "Pizzeria Uno is a chain. Why go there?" she told me once. "Go to the Duck & Bunny." When I stopped giggling over the name, I went to the Duck & Bunny, a quaint little eatery in Providence's Fox Point neighborhood. I loved their crepes. Sadly, the owners closed Duck & Bunny in 2019, and it became a pile of rubble two years later.

In 2018, Austrian company THQ Nordic acquired the rights to the one video game Schilling's company actually did produce, "Kingdoms of Amalur: Reckoning," and released it two years later. That money went toward paying down the debt.

In spring 2022 state officials released a complex $220 million plan to renovate the "Superman Building," the long-vacant Art Deco office tower in downtown Providence that resembled the building shown on the Superman television shows of the 1950s. Skeptics invoked the 38 Studios debacle. "Big projects with big taxpayer subsidies deserve big-time transparency," the website GoLocalProv editorialized.

Schilling, despite a sparkling 20-year career that included an 11-2 postseason record and sharing 2001 World Series Most Valuable Player honors with Arizona Diamondbacks teammate Randy Johnson, has failed to make the Hall of Fame. He missed in 2022 on his 10th try to reach the 70% voter threshold that the Baseball Writers' Association of America established. Still, Schilling could make the hall through alternative means, namely a veterans' selection committee.

"Numerous public comments, expressing not really political points as much as messages of hate and intolerance, put him in this hot water," Ken Davidoff wrote in the New York Post. "While Schilling voiced many thoughts as a player, especially once he shined on Boston's big stage, leading the 2004 Red Sox to their first championship since 1918, he considerably amped up his toxicity after he stopped pitching."

In social media posts, Schilling compared Muslims to Nazis and joked about lynching journalists. ESPN fired him as a baseball commenter after an antitransgender rant. He also collected Nazi memorabilia.

"He was an outspoken team leader, frequent sparring partner with the media and a larger-than-life personality, especially in the postseason," Steve Gardner wrote in USA Today. "Despite being one of the best pitchers of his generation, Schilling's greatest barrier to Cooperstown may be his public persona since his playing days ended."

As for 38 Studios, "It's still a black eye for Rhode Island. But the nice thing about black eyes is that they go away. And you can learn to duck the next time," said Anthony Sabino, a St. John's University law professor.

Rhode Island, he said, needed to stand up to any celebrity. "Curt Schilling, Kim Kardashian, anyone — and if they say, 'I want a hundred million,' [the state] could say, 'Uh-uh.'"

Love that dirty water

How it all began in hometown Boston

Fittingly, one of my final podcast guests before I retired was Larry DiCara, a Boston historian, bond lawyer and former politician. It marked a nice bookend to my career.

DiCara was a gadfly Boston City Council member right out of Harvard University in the early 1970s when I was a 19-year-old covering City Hall for the Boston Ledger, a downtown weekly. We built a rapport as the young'uns in our respective endeavors. "It was a great time to be in city government, and, truth be told, the rest of life has been relatively easy," he said on my show.

We discussed how Boston had changed over the years, with the 2021 mayoral election as the backdrop. An Asian-American, Michelle Wu, defeated fellow City Council member Annissa Essaibi George, of Turkish descent, in the November runoff. Wu's predecessor, acting mayor Kim Janey, was the city's first black and female mayor, filling the open slot when Marty Walsh resigned to become President Biden's labor secretary.

"Every significant candidate was identified as a person of color, and the four top [primary] finishers were women," said DiCara, who spent 10 years on the City Council in the 1970s and 1980s and was acting mayor during the infamous Blizzard of 1978, when Mayor Kevin White couldn't get back from his Florida vacation.

DiCara also wrote the book, "Turmoil and Transition in Boston: A Political Memoir from the Busing Era." Federal Judge W. Arthur Garrity Jr.'s order in June 1974 mandated racial busing in the city's public schools. His remedies for what he determined was a segregated school system wrought chaos in the city and triggered some violence. It gave Boston some bad national media exposure. Incidents included a stabbing at South Boston High, a mob chasing a black man out of his car and the ugly sight of someone using the pointed end of an American flag as a weapon against another minority. Nearly 50 years later, a play called "Common Ground Revisited," based on a book about the busing crisis, ran locally at the Huntington Theatre.

In the 1970s, the City Council consisted of nine members, all elected at-large or citywide. Under the city's strong-mayor, weak-council system, the council's powers were limited, especially under Mayor Kevin White, who took the strong-mayor description seriously. Voters in 1981 approved a measure expanding the council to 13 members, nine by district and four at-large. The old nine-member council often featured a 5-4 split between males of Irish and Italian descent. Outliers included Tom Atkins, an African-American, and Louise Day Hicks, a two-time mayoral candidate and later a congresswoman, known nationally for her pushback on school busing. She was from the South Boston neighborhood central to the busing opposition.

Also on the council was Albert "Dapper" O'Neil, a two-fisted sort who often generated headlines. DiCara in his book called him "a crass Irish-American hack who could be counted on to denigrate women, gays, minorities and anyone else he decided to hate that day. I think it is safe to say that Dapper didn't like me much, but then he hated everyone."

I vividly recall one council budget meeting in a City Hall conference room in which Dapper let loose on Paul Parks, a black administrator of Boston's Model Cities program who later became state education commissioner. Parks was also a combat engineer who joined U.S. armed forces crossing the English Channel into Normandy during World War II. Dapper did an overhead slam of the city's budget book, which was the size of two yellow-pages books, and invoked the pejorative "you people" when shouting at Parks. When Dapper spoke in the council chambers, the press row was in his direct sight. He could see us when we snickered at his rants and often interjected, "And if I'm humoring anyone …"

Once when Dapper was riding in Dorchester past a cluster of Vietnamese businesses, he remarked: "I thought I was in Saigon, for chrissakes." He tried to brush it off later by saying he was talking about "letting bygones be bygones."

Council President Gerald O'Leary once told me he liked using the restroom at the downtown Park Plaza hotel bar — where my late father, Harold, worked for 25 years — because he could grab peanuts out of the bowl on the way. When Dad found out, he had the bowl ready: "Here you go, councilor." Later, O'Leary was involved with a lot more than peanuts. A federal judge in 1981 sentenced O'Leary, after he became a school committee member, to 18 months for trying to extort $650,000 from a firm hired to bus students under the desegregation program. Small world, by the way: My company for a few years hosted conferences at the Park Plaza, and at least one happy-hour reception bartender fondly remembered Dad.

Political rogues abounded in Boston. In one series of hearings I covered, the watchdog Finance Commission, or FinCom, focused on the pressure school department employees felt to buy tickets to testimonial fund-raisers elected school committee members would hold. "Things like pay raises — I didn't want to be forgotten," said one skittish career desk jockey. The school committee wielded influence way beyond education. At one hearing a public speaker complained that only two of the five school committee members helped him oppose a liquor license. "Why would a school committee member get involved with liquor licenses?" I naively asked a fellow reporter. I was a cub at the time, remember. His response: "Don't kid yourself."

I made shitty pay at the time, but covering City Hall was a terrific experience. Despite the lousy pay, I managed to repeatedly stuff my face with crabmeat sandwiches at the iconic Union Oyster House behind City Hall. Other media, which included Bob Jordan of the Globe, Janice Elliott of the Herald and Brad Knickerbocker of the Christian Science Monitor, welcomed me as a colleague. I also enjoyed chatting with well-known TV hands Arch McDonald and Walt Sanders, the latter one of the few black TV journalists in the city at the time. Knickerbocker let me ride with him on election night in 1973. We went from City Hall out to West Roxbury, on the city's southern extremity, to cover the election of upstart council candidate James Michael Connolly. The election-night experience was invaluable.

Despite the ugliness of the 1970s, Boston, in later years, has gotten an unfair rap about race. My alma mater, Brighton High School, was one of the few racially mixed high schools in the city at the time with 35% minority, and the memories are all positive. But I was glad I got out two years before the busing order and its resultant chaos. UMass-Boston, where I attended college, was also racially mixed and conflict-free. Too many people today overplay the race card. The once-brilliant Boston Globe newspaper has become a cauldron of wokeish race-baiting with the likes of columnist Renee Graham frequently stirring the pot. While Boston has had its share of racial problems — I'll never forget the Registry of Motor Vehicles staffers who kept calling an older black man "shithead" — the "Boston is racist" mantra has become cheap editorial currency of late.

Owen McNamara was my initial editor and a mentor. When I was a Brighton High senior, he liked my submittals to the local Allston-Brighton Citizen Item, part of the Citizen Group Publications chain in Brookline that included the Boston Ledger. TV legends Mike Wallace and David Susskind cut their teeth there. After Owen played up my stories about a Brighton High football team that won a rare District League championship, he called me over to his newsroom and encouraged me to branch out beyond sports. That resulted in high school officials creating an internship for me even though the school had no formal internship program. For that I'm forever grateful.

I also got my first glimpse of the kind of nasty office politics all too common in journalism: Owen left because the family that owned the newspaper chain offered his job to someone else behind his back. One of the creepiest moments I experienced over my 45-year career was the sight of patriarch G. Russell Phinney coming into the newsroom and unwrinkling pieces of paper out of a wastebasket to read what was on them. Owen was hospitalized with surgery at the time. The silence in the room was deafening. Owen eventually capped off his excellent career editing Boston University's medical publications. After he died, the New England Society for Healthcare Communications created the Owen J. McNamara Excellence in Writing Award. I was always proud to call myself an Owen McNamara protégé.

Later in the 1970s, Boston experienced the Blizzard of 1978. It was my first winter living in Hartford, Connecticut, and when the storm hit, I spent three nights sleeping on my desk in my suburban office. On the first night, Monday, Feb. 6, I barely got a Boston radio station and listened to the Beanpot college hockey tournament. The city was officially closed, but nearly 12,000 people still made it to the old Boston Garden for the doubleheader. Many had to stay inside the Garden for four days, subsisting on leftover hot dogs.

"I know a lot of people of my vintage sort of look back whimsically as if it were Woodstock with snow," DiCara said on my podcast. "And certainly, lots of people ended up sleeping at places other than their residences. But it was a crisis for the city. We had to rescue a lot of people. Ambulances had trouble getting down the street. And, for our young listeners, there were no emails, there were no cellphones."

In my Bond Buyer years, I gave extensive coverage to the controversies around the Massachusetts Bay Transportation Authority (MBTA) employee pension fund. The MBTA Retirement Fund operates separately from the state-run MBTA, which operates Greater Boston's mass-transit system. Bolstered by state court rulings in its favor, the fund has operated as a private trust since its founding in 1948. Fund officials have long fought the efforts of open-government advocates, including Boston think tank Pioneer Institute, who want to open its books. It holds its meetings in private and has shut out media from them.

A Pioneer report in 2014 said cronyism and "endemic" conflicts of interest made the fund a cautionary tale for institutional investors. In 2013 the MBTA itself released some data that showed 17% of 6,359 listed former employees retired from the transit system while in their

40s. Published reports also connected the fund's dealings to associates of convicted mass murderer James "Whitey" Bulger and Francis Fraine, a Bulger associate who admitted to a role in a frightening Back Bay arson ring in the late 1970s. The Retirement Fund also lost an estimated $25 million investment in an apparent Ponzi scheme through a hedge fund run by Fletcher Asset Management.

As the coronavirus pandemic hit, radio station WBUR's Beth Healy reported that despite promises of reform from Gov. Charlie Baker and others, "the T's pension board is still secretive and has agreed to move only a sliver of its money — less than 1% — to the state retirement manager."

A report for Pioneer in 2022 by E.J. McMahon, founding senior fellow of the Empire Center for Public Policy in Albany, New York, estimated the fund's long-term pension liability at $1.3 billion, or nearly triple the MBTA's total payroll. McMahon advised the MBTA to not issue $360 million in pension obligation bonds, calling such a move "a wrong turn at the worst possible time." He added, "It would be much like taking out a home equity loan to pay off a credit card cash balance, without generating any meaningful structural reforms that are needed to fix the actual issues."

Wu took office in November 2021, generating national headlines.

"It seems as though the demographics of the political class in Boston have caught up with the demographics of the city," said Providence College political science professor Adam Myers. "For me, it's been interesting to observe the dynamics of this mayoral race."

Wu was one of the few progressives who did well locally that fall. In Buffalo, India Walton, who had defeated four-term incumbent Byron Brown in a Democratic primary in June, lost badly to Brown in November as she tried to become the first self-declared socialist mayor since Milwaukee's Frank Zeidler in 1960. Brown generated a write-in campaign to get another shot at Walton. Results in Minneapolis and Seattle, meanwhile, reflected opposition to defunding-the-police measures and mass decriminalization.

Wu's learning curve has included the need to realize a mayor's limits. Central to her campaign was a call for free rides on Boston-area transit, which was not her call since the state operates the MBTA. "I think Michelle has to balance her zeal for dramatic change with the realities of the world as we know it," DiCara said. Wu has been misguided in labeling people who opposed her vaccine mandates as haters and in her insistence on a neighborhood-specific $7,500 fee for North End restaurateurs to participate in outdoor dining. The latter sparked a lawsuit from the businesses. And her reference to "food security" needs in the context of off-road-vehicle flash mobs harassing motorists on city streets was lame.

While I consider Wu's politics overly hard left, I must admit her approach to the transit-fare issue has been shrewd. Sidestepping the state, she shepherded the use of $8 million of federal pandemic rescue funds to backstop free rides on three bus routes covering poorer neighborhoods for two years. She has also been seeking agreements from some neighboring communities on common bus routes. Transit advocates outside Massachusetts have taken notice, including New York, where the "Fair Fares" discount program has been a political football for several years.

"Mass and Cass," the opioid corridor along Massachusetts Avenue and Melnea Cass Boulevard near Boston Medical Center in the South End, is an ongoing problem despite Wu's attempts to clear homeless encampments by relocating that population to temporary housing. According to local media, hundreds removed from the area have since returned, with drug use and crime still major problems for both Mass and Cass, and adjacent neighborhoods Roxbury, Dorchester and South Boston. Wu, meanwhile, had to wrestle with a more empowered City Council to minimize the council's cuts to the police overtime budget.

Meanwhile, loud predawn protests outside her Roslindale home prompted legislation by Wu to limit hours of such gatherings. The City Council passed the ordinance in March 2022. Good, I say. Dislike her politics if you want, but this is a quality-of-life measure that will benefit the city overall. A Boston Herald editorial called the home-picketing ban, while self-serving for Wu, "a boon for all Bostonians." The Herald, often critical of the mayor, added: "Wu's ordinance doesn't remove the right to protest and demonstrate — it just returns some much-needed civility to the equation."

A study in contrasts

Connecticut is home to massive wealth and urban poverty

Connecticut has some of the nation's highest wealth metrics, and some very poor cities. Contrasts always make good storylines.

"The gap between its richest and poorest citizens — and that between the top and the middle class — outstrips those in most other states, and in many other corners of the globe," Keith Phaneuf wrote in the Connecticut Mirror.

In September 2017 I drove to Hartford to cover a fiscally shaky state and its wobbly capital city. Call it a one-stop shop. Connecticut's budget was three months late while Hartford was flirting with bankruptcy. Compelling drama.

Having lived in Hartford for 11 years, I always liked visiting there. Earlier in my career, I covered state politics and gubernatorial campaigns and interviewed Gov. Ella Grasso — the first woman elected governor on her own merit — at her family home in Windsor Locks. As the editor-in-chief of Hartford Sports Extra magazine, I doubled up as a hockey columnist, covering the National Hockey League's Whalers throughout several eastern U.S. and Canadian cities. I also called high school sports play-by-play on commercial AM radio and local-origination cable. Additionally, I did commentaries and between-period interviews on Yale University men's hockey broadcasts on New Haven's WELI radio.

Connecticut's legislature was in session, and I was also to interview Hartford Mayor Luke Bronin. I did sit-down and phone interviews with Bronin before and got some sound bites from him at a Brookings Institution public-finance conference in Washington.

Bronin, a former general counsel under Gov. Dannel Malloy, struck me as a straight shooter, glib and candid. He took office in January 2016 and found the city's finances much more severe than predecessor Pedro Segarra had led him to believe. "When I got here, I looked under the hood, and it was worse than I had imagined," Bronin once said.

But this day, Bronin canceled my appointment at the last minute. His chief of staff, Vas Srivastava, called me while I was about 45 minutes out, asking what I planned to bring up in the interview. I sensed something was brewing. "Is the appointment still on?" I asked. He said yes. But when I got to City Hall, Vas came out to the mayor's office reception area and said without elaborating, sorry, the mayor had to cancel.

At the State Capitol, I caught the end of a legislative hearing and met up with state Sen. Scott Frantz, a Republican who represented Greenwich from 2009 to 2018 and chaired the finance, revenue and bonding committee. Frantz was a good contact. He would occasionally take the train from Greenwich, where he was president of investment firm Haebler Capital, to our Lower Manhattan newsroom to record a video or podcast.

"I have to attend a caucus, but consider this your home away from home," Frantz said as we went into his office. "Feel free to make yourself comfortable and set up here."

When I opened up my laptop, I got an eyeful. S&P dropped Hartford's bond rating further into junk status, lowering it four notches to B-minus from BB. It marked the latest action from Wall Street, which was pile-driving the city's standing in the capital markets. Suddenly I was playing messenger, emailing the news to top lawmakers while seeking reactions. Then Frantz came back to the office. "Got your email," he said. "Holy shit."

The next day I covered a UConn School of Law conference on municipal distress. Bronin spoke but told the media afterward he really couldn't reveal much. As it turned out, the mayor was in delicate negotiations with bondholders and other parties.

People at the conference were constantly checking their smartphones for developments at the capitol. Three Democrats in a state Senate already split 18-18 along party lines broke ranks and sided with Republicans to reject the latest budget proposal. Six weeks later, and after more haggling, Connecticut's budget finally passed.

In Hartford, which hugs the west bank of the Connecticut River, city debt per capita was spiking while the city's reserve fund balance was plummeting. Population and business were both in sharp decline. Notably, iconic insurer Aetna was threatening to leave its Farmington Avenue headquarters for New York. CVS Health Corp. avoided such a move when it bought Aetna for $69 billion in 2018, saying it would keep the company in its home since 1853.

In addition, half the capital city's property is tax-free, thus stunting revenue. Thanks to the plethora of state buildings, hospitals, colleges, Metropolitan District Commission facilities and nonprofits, Hartford — geographically tiny to begin with at only 18 square miles — has 35% less taxable property than prosperous neighbor West Hartford and barely more taxable property than small, affluent suburbs Farmington and Glastonbury.

"Cities in Connecticut do not just face a fiscal crisis; they have a deeper crisis rooted in market irrelevance and social isolation," Bruce Katz wrote in a Brookings Institution op-ed that resonates 20 years later. "Hartford's decline is partly a reflection of state laws and practices that subsidize sprawl and permit suburbs to wall themselves off from regional responsibilities."

Bronin frequently called for regional solutions such as shared municipal services. He spoke frequently at town-hall type sessions that included the suburbs. The climb was uphill. "We are a city with the tax base of a suburb," he said.

In spring 2018 the state and city crafted a bailout agreement. As part of an oversight plan, it called for Connecticut to take over the city's roughly $540 million of debt.

Connecticut never embraced its cities, and years later, it missed out on the "back to the city" thrust. Insurance company employees would flee to the suburbs right after work, except to attend UConn basketball or Whalers hockey games, or maybe a Hartford Stage Company performance. The NHL's Whalers left for Carolina after the 1996–97 season.

"People didn't typically visit Hartford," Tim Rohan wrote in Sports Illustrated. "They passed through on their way to Boston or New York. Hartford's main attraction was the Mark Twain House."

Negative city stereotypes lingered. But the South End, where I settled for a decade after moving from Boston in 1977, was a vibrant, heavily Italian-American neighborhood. While hardly pristine, it was agreeable. Its weekend "festa" every September drew more than 1 million people on Franklin Avenue, way more than that thoroughfare could handle. But the recession of 2008 hit that neighborhood hard, and it has fallen on difficult times.

Insurance executives generally settled in the region's affluent suburbs west of the river, including West Hartford, Farmington, Avon and Simsbury, while east of the river, where East Hartford-based defense contractor Pratt & Whitney was a major employer, higher earners chose the likes of South Windsor and Manchester.

The University of Connecticut was another force. Institutionally it was the 800-pound gorilla that usually got what it wanted. In sports it was UConn, first, last and always. The Huskies have won multiple national titles in women's and men's basketball, and their omnipresence helped grease the path for the hockey Whalers' exit.

UConn was even part of the backdrop when state officials wooed the National Football League's New England Patriots in 1998. When the Patriots looked to relocate from Foxboro, Massachusetts, the state legislature was prepared to fund a stadium. UConn's fight song blared at a rally for the Pats in downtown Hartford. Then-Gov. John Rowland offered for the state to pay the entire cost of the stadium, estimated at $374 million, and — according to Rohan — team owner Robert Kraft would have gotten any leftover money.

While ostensibly the move was designed to put the city on the sports map big-time and compensate for the loss of the Whalers, it was also a back-door means to stroke UConn by providing it a football stadium. "I'm glad that we're going to get the Patriots, but part of me doesn't like seeing UConn getting its own way again," a non-UConn college sports information director told me at a basketball game.

The Hartford project stalled amid logistics problems with the site, that of the Hartford Steam Plant. Kraft still wanted a stadium in Hartford, near downtown and the interstates. Instead, he accepted a counteroffer early in 1999 from Massachusetts officials. The Patriots remained in Foxboro, built Gillette Stadium and won six Super Bowl championships. UConn instead got a scaled-down Rentschler Field in East Hartford, essentially a consolation prize. The football program has struggled in its move to big time. Over five seasons through 2021, the Huskies lost 50 of 60 games.

"The Patriots got a new venue in [Foxboro], and Hartford got ... a college football stadium across the river and some hurt feelings to go along with it," Alex Putterman wrote in the Hartford Courant.

Hartford, sadly, never tapped its waterfront as a resource until recent years. North-south Interstate 91 effectively divided downtown from the river. Exhibit A of highway-design convolution was the interchange of I-91 and east-west I-84. Urban legend, never really denied, had the late businesswoman Beatrice Fox Auerbach threatening to move her flagship G. Fox & Co. department store to the suburbs unless a highway exit funneled traffic near the store and a parking garage. G. Fox closed that store in 1993, and the company ultimately got subsumed into Boston's Filene's and then New York–based Macy's. Its downtown site is now a mixed-use parcel.

Three of the eight possible connections between I-91 and I-84 back then involved crawling through local streets. I-84, meanwhile, cut off a swath of downtown just north of the highway, adjacent to the blighted North End. It was no-man's land until the minor-league baseball Dunkin' Donuts Park opened in 2017.

Hartford was an insurance town. "Mother Aetna," the Travelers, the Hartford, Cigna and Phoenix Mutual all set up shop there once. You tried to avoid "Aetnoid" parties. Shop talk about who got transferred to Chicago tends to ruin a fun night. Likewise, Hartford — and Connecticut as a whole — had trouble letting down their collective hair. It's an inevitability when your dominant employer is insurance, an industry that calculates probability of disaster.

Tolling to this day has been a political football. The state in the 1980s removed tolls on the Connecticut Turnpike — I-95 west of New Haven — after a 1983 Stratford tollgate crash killed seven people. Later that year, another disaster happened on I-95. A 100-foot-long section of the Mianus River Bridge in Cos Cob, a part of Greenwich, collapsed. Two tractor-trailer trucks and two passenger cars plunged into the river, killing three and injuring three. I considered myself lucky; I briefly considered attending a Yankees-Orioles baseball game in the Bronx that night but dropped the idea. I could have been driving near that bridge on the way back.

The two catastrophes shaped Connecticut infrastructure debate for years.

Small-to-medium media outlets, including my own, had to frequently swim upstream because all that seemed to matter to many people were the Hartford Courant, WSFB-Ch. 3 and WTIC radio. A sense of entitlement festered among those three. For instance, Ch. 3 reporter Celeste Ford, who later worked for New York's Ch. 7, threw a major hissy fit when state officials didn't time their toll-closing ceremony with her live spot. Staff from smaller outlets, meanwhile, faced a double whammy of having to battle for respect internally. "We worked hard and did a lot of creative things and the higher-ups didn't give a damn," a former radio station manager said — gee, that sounds familiar — after leaving to handle public relations for a nonprofit.

In recent times Connecticut's revenue woes prompted renewed calls for tolling. Debate over congestion pricing, a hot-button but stalled issue for New York City, even surfaced in Connecticut. State transportation officials said studies of I-95 along southwest Connecticut and

I-84 in Hartford show the state could generate roughly $750 million per year through the initiative.

Neighboring states have toll roads and proponents say electronic tolling would diffuse safety objections. Opponents cited a possible worsening of local road conditions thanks to motorists circumventing the toll gantries, plus a wariness of how the state would manage the money.

"It's the words 'toll' and 'trust in government' that make people pause and say, 'You know what? This plan is scary in a lot of ways,'" said Len Fasano, a Republican Senate minority leader from North Haven through 2020 and now a legislative commissioner in the state legislature.

One politician I admired was Kevin Lembo, the state comptroller from 2011 to 2021 before resigning due to a heart illness. Lembo, a Democrat who earned respect from both sides of the aisle, would call out officials over everything from budget imbalance to budgetary bickering, which he said jeopardized Connecticut's standing on Wall Street.

"When the economy surges and state revenue rises with it, new, sometimes costly programs are created. In Connecticut our 169 towns compete for bond funding, lining up to get gazebos and band shells, and they often get handed out in good economic times, like candy at trick-or-treat time," he told me after a September 2016 speech before the Municipal Analysts Group of New York at the Yale Club in Manhattan. MAGNY officials piously labeled his speech off the record, yet Lembo sang me an opera afterward, my recorder in hand. I ran fully with his comments.

Both sides of Connecticut's political aisle respected me. Republican Frantz said the media needed more people like me on the ground, while state Treasurer Shawn Wooden, a progressive Democrat, called me "highly engaging for a business journalist."

Connecticut's budget picture was brighter at the end of 2021. The state took steps to boost its budgetary reserves and offset its pension liability and received across-the-board bond-rating upgrades from Moody's, S&P, Fitch and Kroll. New Yorkers, thanks to factors such as rising urban crime, COVID infection rates, the work-at-home dynamic and the desire for more open space, have been trickling into the state.

"We've always seen buyers from New York City," Stephanie Phillips, a real estate agent with Houlihan Lawrence in Darien, told the Connecticut Insider. "I think as a lot of the businesses continue to let their employees work remotely, or at the very least part time, a lot of clients are coming out from the city and saying, 'Well, I can manage a commute two days a week, and that's not bad.' They're looking for more space, as well, so it's a good tradeoff."

Yet COVID-19 shined an even harsher light on the rich-poor gap. According to a survey by the advocacy organization DataHaven, about a quarter of adults who live in urban communities struggled with economic and food security. By contrast, more than a third of those who earn more than $100,000 reported being better off financially than in February 2020.

"The survey shows that adults in Connecticut's urban areas endured more pandemic-related hardships than their suburban counterparts," said DataHaven Executive Director Mark Abraham.

The spoken word

From podcasts to play-by-play, the voice is your own

S hortly before we started our podcast series at the Bond Buyer, I was in Rhode Island chatting with a banking source.

"Whatever you do, don't make your show an NPR snoozer," he told me in a clear swipe at National Public Radio's programming.

Three months later, I was on the phone with him.

"John, I lived up to my promise. No NPR snoozers," I said.

He replied, "Funny you mention NPR. Last week I was on one of their shows, and 10 minutes in, I wished the hell I wasn't on it."

Hosting podcasts was natural for me. While much of my publishing career involved print, I had appeared on national TV and radio, notably former CBS News correspondent Sharyl Attkisson's syndicated documentary program "Full Measure," on which I discussed public debt. I also had done sports play-by-play on commercial AM radio in Connecticut and anchored the sports segment of a national, award-winning newscast on local-origination cable.

Further, I had moderated conference panels for multiple companies and was a periodic guest lecturer at universities and prep schools, notably Villanova School of Business outside Philadelphia and Kingswood Oxford School in West Hartford, Connecticut. The respective lecturers, David Fiorenza at Villanova and Rob Kyff at K-O, enjoyed having me there. So did the students.

The voice is yours, not that of some nondescript desk editor.

The podcasts evolved from our popular short videos. To get the series up and running, editor-in-chief Mike Scarchilli had to circumvent one of his own bosses, pitching the other during vacation season. We had internal politics at play. Scarchilli then told me he really wanted to make a big bang with our opening show.

"I have a two-word answer for you," I said. "Dick Ravitch."

Richard Ravitch was a New York City power broker for more than 50 years. He played a major role in guiding the city out of its financial crisis in the 1970s. A few years later, as chairman of the Metropolitan Transportation Authority, he lobbied state officials to approve the MTA's first five-year capital program, enabling it to borrow billions of dollars to cover a huge repair backlog. Ravitch ran unsuccessfully for mayor and was briefly the state's lieutenant governor under David Paterson. In his later years, Ravitch advised on the Detroit and Puerto Rico bankruptcies and was a director at the Volcker Alliance, a think tank founded by former Federal Reserve Chairman Paul Volcker.

Ravitch was a news magnet. "Hey guys, Ravitch is on the public speakers list," former Daily News writer Pete Donahue once told fellow transit media before an MTA board meeting. People's faces lit up. Ravitch always drew a reaction, whether you agreed with him or not. Dick's booming voice, blunt persona and easy media accessibility made him our ideal opening guest. He always liked the Bond Buyer and me personally. "I'd be happy to, don't mention it," he said at a conference in Boston when I approached him.

The 25-minute show was a big hit. All you had to do is say "hi, Dick," and the rest took care of itself.

"That was great. That was vintage Ravitch. … 'I talked to Horowitz in 1981 …'" Carol Kellermann, then the president of the watchdog Citizens Budget Commission, told me at a CBC breakfast in Midtown Manhattan. Her impersonation of him was pretty good, by the way.

We interviewed politicians, municipal bond analysts, budget watchdogs, transit advocates and former presidential cabinet members. We held frequent, insightful chats about New York City's budget that included Maria Doulis and later Andrew Rein from the Citizens

Budget Commission, and Howard Cure, director of municipal bond research for Evercore Wealth Management. Doulis, later a deputy to New York State Comptroller Tom DiNapoli, called herself a "budget wonk" on social media but didn't talk like one. She was chatty and easy to understand. Booking her repeatedly was a no-brainer. Likewise, Cure interweaved deep fiscal analysis with sharp political context, all straightforward. Good stuff. Colleague Chip Barnett and I also baked in some video spots, including budget coverage from the City Hall rotunda.

Three-way interviews, which had me skeptical at first, proved a big hit. You just have to do them right so people won't bump into each other when they talk. The host is a traffic cop of sorts. Andrew Coen and I moderated transit discussions that included outside guests Nicole Gelinas from the Manhattan Institute for Policy Research, and Nick Sifuentes from the Tri-State Transportation Campaign. The topics were heavy, but the banter was jovial, making it win-win all around.

Other popular guests included "Hurricane Czar" Alan Rubin, a public-finance attorney who talked like everyone's favorite uncle as he simplified climate-change complexities. New York City transportation commissioner Polly Trottenberg, now U.S. deputy secretary of trans-portation, was equal parts knowledgeable and glib. Rodney Slater, who was U.S. transportation secretary in the 1990s as part of President Clinton's cabinet and later a partner with law firm Squire Patton Boggs, opened my show with a profound reference to philosopher Henry David Thoreau before diving into national infrastructure matters.

We also had some insightful state fiscal officers on the air. Each brought something to the table. DiNapoli advocated enhanced finan-cial disclosure. Rhode Island Treasurer Seth Magaziner fought for fiscal literacy programs in the state's school systems. His Connecticut peer, Shawn Wooden, pushed for "baby bonds," both in-state and nation-ally. And as part of our live video series, Maine Treasurer Henry Beck spoke of his state's financial strategies while invoking New England and national backdrops.

My "get out there" creed also applied to podcasts. I did the first on-location show during our winter conference at a Midtown Manhattan hotel, then took the series out of town. Fiorenza and I co-hosted multiple programs at Villanova and fielded some sharp questions from his students. Fiorenza now does a weekly podcast with KYW-AM radio in Philadelphia with host Matt Leon, an outgrowth of our in-school shows.

Not far from that campus, I did a segment about a municipal bond analyst survey at the Berwyn, Pennsylvania, home of Tom Kozlik, now the head of research and analytics with Hilltop Securities in the Dallas area and a frequent guest on national business networks. And in Providence, Rhode Island, I recorded an impromptu show with Henry Cisneros, also a former Clinton cabinet member as secretary of Housing and Urban Development and later an executive at a public finance firm.

Our in-house multimedia personnel, notably Kellie Malone and Wen-Wyst Jeanmary, were first-rate. They were thorough, patient and pleasant. And when the pandemic hit, I simply broadcast from my third-floor study at home, white-knuckling it when the leaf-blower brigade hit our street.

Each show had its own identity, even within our own publication. No two shows were alike, and that was the beauty of it. John Hallacy, a Bond Buyer op-ed commentator and a municipal bond veteran, hosted deep-in-the-weeds analytical shows. Mine were a little looser. Both of us were effective. John and I also co-hosted podcasts occasionally, including a reminiscence about New York financial power broker Felix Rohatyn shortly after he died. Sister publications followed suit and before long, podcasts ran company-wide.

"The audio work that you did for this brand and this company was pioneering," Scarchilli told me when I retired. "The work you did on Future of Cities last year, for example, helped set a template we can use for special projects."

Our four-part Future of Cities series, which evolved during the pandemic, ran in the fall of 2020 with a handful of editors, including myself, participating. We won a national first-place Neal Award from the Software & Information Industry Association for best subject-related package in business-to-business journalism. I hosted a companion narrative podcast for each of the four segments — how cities can survive; inflection points for businesses; the "gathering economy," i.e., sports and entertainment; and resilience amid urban unrest, budget strife and climate volatility. The podcasts essentially carried the series, bringing the whole package to life. It was my fourth national or state award overall and first outside sports, though sports was a small component of this one.

I opened the series with a live video that featured Cisneros with Tom Wright, president of transportation-themed think tank Regional Plan Association. In the planning stage, we briefly thought of asking New York Gov. Andrew Cuomo to appear, but dismissed the idea within seconds. The egomaniacal Cuomo and his people would have tried to dictate the interview terms.

Future of Cities did indeed provide a blueprint. I patterned my special two-part series on the June 2021 New York City mayoral primary accordingly. Ditto for another two-parter three months later on the 20th anniversary of the Sept. 11 attacks.

Even just before retirement, when I hated my job because of the overwork and the office politics, I loved the podcasts. My final guests included Katherine Craven, chief administrative and financial officer at Babson College in suburban Boston and one of the most astute public-finance leaders in the U.S. Northeast. We discussed the national outlook for higher education amid the pandemic.

Pick the right guests and you're ahead of the game, regardless of your level of broadcast experience or speaking voice. I avoided bond rating analysts — the folks from Moody's, S&P, Fitch and Kroll. Overly measured people are tedious. Further, they wanted their questions verbatim in advance. If you need us to spoon-feed you your questions ahead of time, you don't belong on my show. Moody's, noted for its institutional arrogance, was especially difficult. Its media-relations flack during much of my stay was smug and condescending. Nobody at the Bond Buyer liked him.

"They take themselves too seriously, seeing themselves as the high priests of credit analysis, making them see decisions as more portentous than they are," one fellow journalist said of Moody's.

Rating agencies have no business being sanctimonious, given their signature mistakes that included investment-grade ratings for shaky credits preceding the mortgage market crisis and also for Puerto Rico, before the island territory spiraled into bankruptcy.

At one conference I covered in Washington, an event organizer came up to me during a panel discussion and whispered: "That Moody's speaker doesn't want to be quoted."

My reply: "He's not worth quoting."

The event planner covered her mouth to stifle laughter.

I held to a "no blind dates" rule for podcasts. Media flacks would frequently pitch potential guests, but I would screen for suitability. Prior media interviews or even YouTube clips were helpful if you didn't know the person directly. Book a reluctant person and you'll get someone who sounds as though he or she has eight things to do and the recording is fifth on the list. I also had a built-in radar while interviewing people for written stories that told me whether they could be good audio/video guests … or not. I eliminated one prospect, someone I knew quite well, because he prefaced an answer during a telephone interview by saying, "Let me see how I can say this without offending anybody." That revealed a lack of spontaneity.

You want to fend off media flacks who are too pushy. One handler for someone who ran around calling himself an "urbanist" wanted an appearance fee for his client and, while expressing that, insulted us. "Since this is not a traditional media outlet, are you offering compensation for his content, expertise and time?" I told him to shove it. The best media flacks are enhancers, not palace guards. I experienced the good, the bad and the ugly among the PR folks. Among the best were Brian Moynihan, Andrea Rodeschini and Jaszver Bauzon from multiple New York law firms; Aaron Donovan from New York MTA; and both April Mason and Christina Forrest from Violet PR, a boutique firm in Montclair, New Jersey. The ugliest may have been someone who put "story pitch" in all capital letters in the subject line … and misspelled pitch. And the most obnoxious people looped in your boss on emails, which always generated an ugly backlash.

At times I moderated panel discussions at our conferences in Philadelphia. They involved half-hour "lightning round" discussions of public-finance issues such as pensions or infrastructure. They were right in my wheelhouse and at day's end, just before the happy-hour reception. We skipped the visual presentations, thank God, and held to our timetable with the help of a countdown clock. People get loopy after a full day of monotones and PowerPoint slides. "Forty-plus years in the media and I'm good at meeting deadlines," I would say. People made their party across the hall in time. That resonated.

I eventually withdrew from moderating because I didn't get to choose my own co-panelists. Conference sponsors cluttered the panels with their own people — the same-old bunch — some who were beyond dull. As football coach Bill Parcells once said, if they expect you to cook the meal, they ought to let you shop for the groceries. I did, however, occasionally work with decent people on those panels. One vibrant session featured Philadelphia Treasurer Jackie Dunn, Tiffany Tribbitt from S&P and Tim Blake, someone at Moody's who actually spoke in clear English. We also added some thought-provoking topics to my panels, including whether a public finance career is advisable to someone coming out of college.

My broadcasting began in November 1980 when I announced on tape delay for a local public-access channel the annual football game in West Hartford, Connecticut, between the town's two public high schools, Hall and Conard. I did color commentary the first half and play-by-play the second, working with Joe DeLuca on a nippy day during which we had to hold down our paper notes in the Hall press box. Conard stopped a late two-point conversion attempt to win an exciting game by one point. "We sounded as though we were on speed," DeLuca told me days later. Still, the telecast was a big hit. The mayor, Nan Streeter, sent us each a complimentary letter. Expectations must have been low. "I attended the game, then watched the telecast at home that night, hoping it would be intelligible," Streeter wrote. She added that "much to [her] surprise and delight," the broadcasting and camera work were commendable.

We added local events such as the West Hartford Classic basketball tournament, which also included private schools Kingswood Oxford and Northwest Catholic. Regionally, we did a high school football game of the week, rotating among Greater Hartford communities within the cable company's franchise. It caught the attention of ESPN announcer Greg Gumbel, later one of the top voices at CBS Sports. Gumbel's daughter was a cheerleader at suburban Simsbury High. When we met at ESPN's five-year celebration up the road in Bristol, Gumbel took a sincere interest in our telecasts, asking me about broadcast-booth positioning and camera angles.

Our broadcast conditions weren't always ideal, but we made it work. With Conard High's press box overly crowded and its view of the field restrictive, we sat atop a production truck in the end zone to call football games. When I worked for Continental Cablevision, whose franchise straddled northern Connecticut and the Springfield, Massachusetts, region, our perch for hockey games at the Enfield Twin Rinks in Connecticut was the roof of the supply shed at the corner of the rink. We dressed up the shed itself with jerseys of the competing teams and did post-game interviews there.

We had our comical moments. During one commercial break at a hockey game that featured the Immaculate High School Mustangs from Danbury, Connecticut, my broadcast partner said to me, "You do know there's no such thing as an immaculate mustang." I had to bite my lip to stifle laughter before we went back on the air. At Enfield High, my colleague had trouble analyzing football replays in the press box because some kid obstructed our 12-inch black-and-white TV monitor while reaching for donuts. The colleague eventually gave up on the replays and turned the monitor to the Michigan State-Notre Dame game on ABC. On one Saturday morning, I had to call a soccer match while lying on the grass. The crew showed up late, some looking groggy. No one provided any chair or table.

Call that character building. The late Vin Scully, the legendary voice of the Brooklyn and Los Angeles Dodgers for 67 seasons, put up with the same stuff as a young pup. His first broadcast was a Maryland-Boston University football game at Fenway Park for CBS Radio in 1949. He dressed lightly and carried loose paper notes despite the late-November chill, only to find out he had to broadcast from the roof, not the enclosed press box. His notes blew away and he ad-libbed as best he could. His bosses at CBS liked how he improvised under the circumstances, and his career took off from there.

Our best Continental broadcast position was the press box, high above ice level, at the Eastern States Coliseum in West Springfield. From there we called hockey games featuring the Springfield Olympics, a junior program that sent players to top-tier Division I colleges. One of them, Bill Guerin, is now a National Hockey League general manager. The "Big E," on fairgrounds that hosted a six-state exposition every fall, was once the home of the World Hockey Association's New England Whalers, later the Hartford Whalers of the NHL and now the Carolina Hurricanes.

In upstate New York, I was a periodic guest on Brian Kenny's late-night "SportsLine Live" talk show on Regional News Network. Kenny, who later succeeded on ESPN and Major League Baseball's MLB Network, frequently had me on to discuss hockey, and I likened NHL commissioner Gary Bettman to "the nerd in high school who would raise his hand and remind the teacher to give out the homework." One summer Kenny had me on to preview the PGA Championship, one of pro golf's Grand Slam events, when Winged Foot Golf Club hosted it in Mamaroneck, New York.

On radio station WCNX in Middletown, Connecticut, I called Middletown, Portland, Cromwell and Xavier high school basketball games. Notable players included Carey Edwards and Chris Smith, who went on to have standout careers at Manhattan College and the University of Connecticut, respectively. We packaged some of our games as parts of doubleheaders that included Central Connecticut State University contests. One Portland-Cromwell game, which Portland won on a shot at the buzzer, played before an overflow crowd at Cromwell akin to scenes from the Indiana-themed movie "Hoosiers." To our benefit, referees often provided us valuable insights about the tendencies of players, coaches and teams at a Hartford bar after Friday night games.

I did post-game summaries of Whalers games for New Haven radio station WELI-AM, for which I also pre-recorded interviews and commentaries for Yale University hockey broadcasts. And as the Whalers had an inspiring playoff run in 1986, I was hosting a Saturday morning show on a Hartford talk-radio station known as WGAB. The call letters were obvious, but the station manager sent a terse memo warning of a one-way trip to Siberia for anyone who spoke of "gab radio." The station, in its own Siberia around 1600 on the AM dial, folded before too long.

One show for WGAB I hosted on the fly, literally. In late April that year, I flew up to Montreal to cover Game 5 of a compelling second-round Stanley Cup playoff series between the Whalers and the Canadiens on a Friday night. Before the game in the afternoon, I did a live spot from my Montreal hotel room and had to turn off the TV because seeing people in barrister wigs during a Parliament session was giving me the sillies. I had to get serious when the station host called and said, "Here's our man in Montreal."

After post-game interviews kept me in the Forum until after midnight, I stayed out a bit late with other media and was hardly in shape to host a show at 11 the following morning back in Hartford. The gravelly voice of Boston Celtics' longtime radio announcer Johnny Most helped wake me up. The basketball team was at an adjacent gate at Boston's Logan Airport, where I was awaiting a connecting flight to Hartford. Most joked loudly about putting star forward Kevin McHale in the baggage compartment.

I made my show on time, and my ace in the hole was guest Emile Francis, the Whalers' general manager. He told me in Montreal the night before when he would be in his office. Francis, who died early in 2022, was well-known in New York as a longtime coach and general manager of the Rangers. Otherwise, much of the three-hour program was a monologue by yours truly. Only two people called in, and one of them was my mother from Boston. I actually addressed her as "caller" before we put her on hold for five minutes of Mutual Broadcasting news, and I had the nerve to say with a straight face, "It's nice to have women fans call our show. Hope we hear from more."

The other caller was a media colleague. "Hi Paul, it's Bill from Waterbury. I hear you loud and clear." Loud and clear from Waterbury? You had trouble hearing us across the street.

Glad we didn't get in trouble with the FCC.

The technoid scourge

How data dweebs are hurting journalism

Bots write news articles. Big Tech crowds out smaller media outlets. Data dweebs outnumber real journalists in many newsrooms.

The technoid scourge has taken hold.

"How do you know I am really a human writing this article and not a robot?" Nicole Martin wrote in Forbes magazine.

Financier Elon Musk's attempted acquisition of Twitter for an estimated $44 billion generated a firestorm, legal and otherwise, and shined a spotlight over Big Tech's influence on the media. Even President Biden's administration has been conveying messages through "influencers" on the social media site TikTok.

Polling of U.S. adults by Schoen Cooperman Research, which News Media Alliance commissioned, revealed extensive worry about tech's effect on local journalism.

"Thousands of local papers have shuttered their doors in recent years, and those surviving are facing unprecedented challenges in remaining both economically viable and as the lifeblood of their communities," pollster Douglas Schoen wrote in the New York Daily News. "All the while, Big Tech monopolies like Alphabet and Meta — through sites like Google News and Facebook News — have come to dominate the news and publishing industries by expropriating the work of smaller and local operators via their news-aggregator sites."

Schoen Cooperman's survey showed that "strong majorities" of Americans — roughly 70% — supported Congress passing a bill called the Journalism Competition and Preservation Act, which would enable news publishers to negotiate fair terms for use of their content by Big Tech companies. The bill includes federal intermediary authority.

News organizations such as Bloomberg and Forbes a few years back began publishing computer-generated stories. "Journalism entered a new phase with the rise of computer-written or automatically produced news articles," five South Korean authors wrote in a collaborative article for Dutch publisher Elsevier.

According to Christina McIntyre, a broadcast journalism lecturer at Glasgow Caledonian University, the Associated Press began producing computer-generated sports and finance stories in 2013, while the Washington Post did likewise with results from the 2016 Summer Olympic Games in Rio de Janeiro, Brazil.

The growth of artificial intelligence, or AI, has many journalists worried about providing the corporate suits another excuse to cut jobs.

"Headline-grabbers they will never be, and for that, journalists should be thankful," McIntyre wrote in an op-ed on The Conversation, a media-oriented website. "The topics are dry and statistics-based, reported in a one-note style which is data-heavy, short on analysis and utterly devoid of color. If it were submitted by one of my journalism students, it's the type of copy I would mark down for being boring."

Sounds like some press releases I used to receive from the Hartford Whalers hockey team. You knew which ones came from the team statistician who was helping out the media-relations department.

Bots are not flawless, the Los Angeles Times higher-ups discovered as they wiped egg off their faces. In June 2017 a Times article falsely reported an earthquake with a 6.8 Richter Scale magnitude had struck Santa Barbara County in California. That earthquake actually happened 92 years earlier. The computer system failed to catch an erroneous notification by the U.S. Geological Survey. The embarrassed Times playfully referred to the "revenge of Y2K" in its correction.

Bots or not, I can relate anecdotally about how the newsroom landscape has changed.

Walk down our corridors — back when people worked in our office — and you would see tech-and-data bureaucrats crawling out of the woodwork like termites. Some were so immersed in their iPhones that you risked bumping into them. Bonafide journalists were down to a precious few. Tech is fine, in the right doses. Technoid bureaucracies are pestilence.

Shortly after our parent company changed from SourceMedia to Arizent — presumably because some focus group thought a tech-like name would attract investors — I asked someone internally about when our new email addresses would take effect and whether I simply hit a button or someone else would handle it.

"Your brand has not migrated yet," she said, astonishingly.

Migrate? What the hell does our brand do, fly south during the winter? English, please.

Internal achievement awards, meanwhile, suddenly went to "content ninjas," "obi wans" and "baby yodas."

So much for being a news organization.

And for all the company's chest-pounding about tech this and tech that, they deleted many of our original podcasts, which pissed off a lot of us. Meanwhile, our website's search engine remained a head-scratcher. A Boolean search for "de Blasio budget," produced the headline: "Wisconsin looks to expand investment banking pools." Look for Providence, the Rhode Island capital, and you'd get: "Hot Springs, Arkansas, seeks to preserve history and revenue." Many of us gave up and looked up our archived articles on Google.

When I simply asked one multimedia person how soon we could create a brief audio clip out of a sound bite, her response was, "I'm not sure what your vision is for this project." What vision? What project? Can you turn this thing around on short notice or not? If you're tied up because you're understaffed and serving all our publications, I understand perfectly. She clarified, apologetically, that her department treats everything as a "project."

Screw the layers of complexity. Just keep it simple. Get story, write (or announce) story and get paid. We need to differentiate between analytics as one tool versus the *only* tool.

Full disclosure: I myself have benefited and embraced many of journalism's technological gains. The growth of the internet in the late 1990s opened up jobs in the industry, and I took advantage of that. And the Bond Buyer's podcast series, subject of a separate chapter in this book, invigorated me late in my career. We also had fun with on-location videos at New York City Hall during budget time. In addition, I designed quick-turnaround graphics while covering budget hearings and briefings. Back in New England, I recorded interviews and commentaries while making some decent supplemental freelance money, for example, doing multimedia work for French-speaking Quebec outlets during pro hockey season. At the editing desk in a New Jersey newspaper, during the formative tech days, we had a breaking-news pager service that a company let us use for free on a trial basis. It alerted us to a major story, the 1999 murder of Orange Police Department inspector Joyce Carnegie. She was the first Essex County female officer and second statewide killed in the line of duty. We rearranged our state page on time and had full coverage.

When I was the sports editor of the Daily Freeman in Kingston, New York, in the 1990s, I wished we had this modern technology. Our terminals were hand-me-downs from the Albany Times Union that were outmoded almost as soon as they arrived. We had no laptops or modems. But we made the best out of it. One night I had reporters simultaneously covering night events in Albany, White Plains and Binghamton. All had to drive back to the Kingston newsroom and write their stories. All made deadline. Our people had situational smarts.

Younger people today have no clue what it's like to have to clang out stories on rickety Royal typewriters and to change your own ribbon before washing your hands, all in the middle of deadline. I started my career that way and don't ever want to go back. Still, we older folks have unfairly had to push back against the dinosaur stereotype. "I'd say that more than any cohort in U.S. history, those over age 50 have had to be more adaptive than any generation before or since, because the bulk of innovation has occurred in our lifetimes," one commenter said online.

Tone-deafness is rampant among the younger tech crowd. At The Deal, where I was a senior editor, a web producer continued to cheerfully yammer about PlayStation video games even after we had all found out a co-worker died. Show some respect. This producer once wrongly posted a story on a Friday afternoon that was embargoed, or "time-stamped," not to appear on our website until the following Monday. He acknowledged the mistake, then strangely argued that he didn't have to embargo anything, not even upon instruction from the editor-in-chief.

Problems with this guy abounded. One Friday he refused to correct a major mistake online, saying he had a train to catch. Never mind that for every minute an error appears on our website, our credibility suffers. And when they gave him the OK to hire some staff, he would read resumes out loud in the newsroom. That job-seeking business reporter from TV station News 12 New Jersey was probably the only such person. So much for confidentiality.

Many news veterans, including those who are tech savvy, have had it. "We had someone 20 years old and bright, but all theory, no sense of the streets," said one whose New York investigative career has spanned print, web and television. "They think they know everything."

L. Stanley "Buddy" Berenson, a pioneer in the parimutuel sport jai alai and the owner of a fronton in Hartford, once told me he'd take someone with street smarts over a Harvard grad with a master's degree. "Geniuses have a way of tripping over their brains," he said.

I advise anyone starting out to speak and write clearly, show interest in other people and listen. And lose the attitude. Trust me, that will put you ahead of the game. In turn, others will respect your input and ideas.

The English language has also sustained collateral damage from the tech epidemic.

Once, when I was scheduled to moderate a conference panel, an event organizer wanted my headshot and biography for the company's brochure. Fine, no problem. But she phrased it, "Please send me your assets." You mean my 401(k)? I need it to retire from this God-awful place. "Sorry, it's 'marketing' speak, or so they say," she said later.

Tech, journalism and social media go hand in hand. Yes, I've been active on Twitter, LinkedIn and Facebook to promote my news coverage and speaking appearances, plus this book and my previous one, "Tales From the Newsrooms." Of the three, I find business networking site LinkedIn the adult in the room. My retirement announcement drew thousands of eyeballs on LinkedIn. Twitter is toxic, no matter who owns it. Facebook has too many people saying their lunch was yummy. But then, it's hard to rant sophomorically about issues of the day on an empty stomach.

"Nothing good happens at 3 in the morning," one media skeptic said. "Social media is 3 in the morning." Case in point is the juvenile sandbox fight on Twitter among Washington Post staffers in mid-2022. Political commentator and comedian Bill Maher called the Post's newsroom "an unlicensed daycare center."

One reporter left her job at a New York City daily because "they focused so much more on getting eyes on their website and Facebook page and videos that I left."

"They stopped caring about news and journalism and only cared about clicks. I get they need clicks to charge advertisers and make money, but they took it too far," she said. "Once they did a photo gallery of [local] elected officials with Snapchat filters on them. So unprofessional and stupid. They always made us do Facebook live videos even though there were no hits to the website and no news value to them. They still do it. … They're less news than they are infotainment on social media. They even changed people's titles from traditional 'reporter' and 'editor' roles to some stupid, newfangled terms like 'content creator' and 'multimedia aggregator.' It's all bullshit and is so frustrating."

One page designer said his newspaper chain has template layouts with preassigned headlines. "It's almost a whole damn story," he said of the headline length. "Lazier editors just use the SEO [search-engine optimization] headline and forget it. So, it's a vicious cycle because the headline writing muscle gets flabby and the design geniuses [sarcasm] keep redesigning pages to be built by people with diminishing skills. Oy vey."

I won't get deep into the weeds here about search-engine optimization or the practice of using "keywords" to make a story more visible in a web search. Safe to say, though, its overemphasis has spawned a parade of self-described "SEO nerds" who have the nerve to call themselves media professionals. The SEO egg-beater has ruined headline writing. Artificial insertions of "keywords" make for awkward headlines, while arcane rules about starting headlines with a subject have encouraged use of the dreaded passive voice.

And pageview story counts can be misleading. I once benefited because my writeup about social impact bonds, which was OK but not terrific, remained front and center on our homepage throughout a long July 4 holiday weekend. People can also manipulate the system. Some writer's demented mother could hit a button 300 times. And at many media companies, pet-favorite staffers often got the before-the-paywall treatment.

Amid rising concerns about Big Tech, one positive thing has emerged. Coverage of tech itself has become less fawning.

"We've been burned," Erin Griffith wrote on the website Wired. "The many hype-building stories about deceptive companies haven't aged well. ... As headlines have exposed the troubling inner workings of company after company, startup culture no longer feels like fodder for gentle parodies about ping pong and hoodies. It feels ugly and rotten."

Yet Martin Bryant wrote in Medium.com that sycophantic coverage of tech in its early days effectively enabled the industry.

"As the tech industry rapidly expanded, boosted in no small part by the growth of smartphones and the app economy, so did the number of media outlets devoted to covering it," Bryant wrote. "These new titles often hired young, inexperienced writers and editors, keen to make an impact in a competitive field. The [media-relations] departments at bigger tech firms used this scrum to their advantage."

Andrew McDiarmid, a senior fellow at the think tank Discovery Institute, called for people to become bosses of their own tech.

"This isn't actually so difficult, but it does require effort," he wrote in the New York Post. "First, win back your mornings and nights. Turn off your gadgets during the first and final hours of the day and give yourself time to think. Second, look for the ways Big Tech is steering your life choices, and then take the wheel and choose for yourself. Third, survey the gadgets, subscriptions and platforms you use regularly. Purge what doesn't positively impact your time, energy, relationships, mind, body and soul."

According to a study by the University of Bath in the United Kingdom, taking a one-week break from social media can lead to significant improvements in well-being, depression and anxiety.

"It took time to demonstrate that cigarettes caused lung cancer," Tim Harford wrote in the Financial Times. "If social media causes depression and anxiety, it will take time to demonstrate that, too. But at this stage, one has to wonder."

There's still hope that newspapers and magazines will remain in some print form, somehow.

"I hope that as a society we don't eventually put all of our eggs into digital. After all, when you're out of battery power or locked out of your account, there's always print," Elyse Major, editor-in-chief at Rhode Island magazine publisher Providence Media, posted on LinkedIn. "You can't get locked out of a magazine."

Close the open office

Let's collaborate and ditch a bad concept

Two years into the COVID-19 pandemic, businesses of all types weighed how workers could return to offices.

"For many, going back to working for the weekend is the nightmare," Tracy Moore wrote in the Washington Post. "Who, exactly, is thirsting to wake up earlier to slog through their commute? Who's excited about team-building exercises, long hours and impromptu meetings?" The pre-pandemic status quo, according to Moore, included "tone-deaf positivity meetings of yore."

I once had the perfect antidote to those meetings when I ran them. I used a countdown clock and a gavel.

While just how many people want to go back instead of working at home is still an open question, one thing is clear: Many don't like dehumanizing open-plan office setups.

If you haven't worked in an open-plan office, you've surely seen or heard about them. Management shoehorns employees onto the same floor. What began as a techie affectation during the dot-com era evolved into a corporate real-estate play. In the public sector, former New York Mayor Michael Bloomberg set up City Hall employees in a "Bloomberg bullpen," an open-plan concept he took from his namesake media company.

Companies cutting back on their real-estate liabilities and laying off workers shoved whatever employees they had left into whatever office space they had left. Workstations often resembled middle-school cafeterias.

Social distancing, in vogue during the pandemic, may help take care of that.

"Clearly there's a new focus now on recalibrating office space consistent with social-distancing best practices," corporate relocation consultant John Boyd Jr. said on my Future of Cities podcast series. "I think you're going to see more momentum for cubicles and a return to what offices looked like 20 years ago, quite frankly."

The coronavirus pandemic probably killed the traditional five-day commute, according to New York Gov. Kathy Hochul. "It may never be a five-day week again," she said. "It may be four days with flexibility. It may be three and a half."

Hochul was still pushing to fill up office buildings "at least three to four days at minimum" to enhance economic recovery. Politicians at all levels have been touting the comeback as an economic-development vehicle. New York City Mayor Eric Adams, meanwhile, said remote work was "draining" recovery in the five boroughs.

Stanford University economics professor Nicholas Bloom, speaking in April 2022 at a conference at the Federal Reserve Bank of New York, said the average New York City office worker intends to reduce office time by nearly 50% and cut annual spending in the city by $6,730, down from an estimated $12,561 before the pandemic took hold.

"Once people have had the chance of not commuting every single day, it's going to be really difficult to get the most talented people to come in for 60 hours a week," Jennifer Glass, a University of Texas professor who has researched telecommuting, told the New York Times. "That's a shift in power. If I were an employer right now, I would not be issuing proclamations about what you won't tolerate."

The Future Forum, a function of workplace-messaging outlet Slack, found an "executive-employee disconnect" about returning to the office in its summer 2022 survey of more than 10,000 workers globally. Two-thirds of executives, according to the study, said they are designing post-pandemic workforce policies with little to no direct input from workers. And 75% of executives say they want to work from the office three to five days a week, compared with only 34% of employees.

"I can't tell you how much I am looking forward to being together again," Apple CEO Tim Cook said in a memo to employees. NBCUniversal chief Jeff Shell was just as saccharine in his own internal note.

There's something odd about these warm-and-fuzzy missives from corporate moguls who over the years have been all too eager to ship jobs overseas.

Remote workers do risk being out of sight, out of mind. "It must be said — and many people won't like this — that the pro-office argument has a lot going for it," Geoff Colvin wrote in Fortune magazine. "When we're together in person, talking face-to-face, the pupils of our eyes constrict and dilate in response to one another. We're not aware it's happening, but research finds that deep in our brains, trust is building."

I've worked at places where the home-office hierarchy condescendingly referred to people based in outer locations as "the remotes." For that reason, I resisted a pre-pandemic offer from the Bond Buyer to work exclusively from my Staten Island home, even though I was already doing that often. I would still sometimes use my office space while in Manhattan covering City Hall, a Metropolitan Transportation Authority board meeting or a business conference. Editor-in-chief Mike Scarchilli, to his credit, never badgered me about where I worked from. He didn't care if I worked from 9 a.m. to 5 p.m., 11 a.m. to 7 p.m., a split shift or whatever, as long as I did the job. He also kept group meetings to a bare minimum.

Amid pandemic developments, still-fluid, major companies have flip-flopped on work-at-home practices. Chief executives Jamie Dimon and David Solomon of JPMorgan Chase and Goldman Sachs, respectively, have been back-to-office stalwarts. Dimon, in an August 2022 interview with Yahoo Finance, called Zoom meetings "management by Hollywood Squares," referring to the old TV game show with the tic-tac-toe setup.

Google and Microsoft were tinkering with hybrid policies, while Amazon was leaving work-from-home policy decisions for its corporate workers up to employee teams rather than workers.

Elon Musk, the chief executive of electric carmaker Tesla and whose on-again, off-again attempt to purchase Twitter has generated international headlines, told employees in June 2022 by email they should return to the office for at least 40 hours per week or leave the company. German unions, among others, are pushing back.

The work-from-homers are asserting themselves in other matters, too, including the movement nationwide to ban or restrict noisy, gas-powered leaf blowers. Those ear-splitting devices are the scourge of many residential areas, including my historic neighborhood. Loud music, from homes and boom cars, is also a big concern.

Companies often packaged the open-office setup as collaboration. It was anything but. Go to any such place and see how many people are wearing headphones to drown out noise. For me, listening to Led Zeppelin's "In the Evening" and "How Many More Times" proved highly effective. Personal space is at a premium. Add that to an often-harrowing and expensive commute amid soaring gas prices, traffic jams, overstuffed buses with large baby strollers blocking the aisles, walkie-talkie cellphone screamers and rubbish on sidewalks. And in major cities, a rash of crimes, notably the April 12, 2022, shooting by a deranged person of at least 10 people on a Brooklyn subway train during rush hour that also left another 19 injured, has many people skittish.

"If keeping real estate costs in check is the priority, leaders should be honest about that with themselves and their employees. Most office redesigns aren't undertaken to promote collaboration," Ethan Bernstein and Ben Waber wrote in a compelling Harvard Business Review research piece that essentially discredited open plans.

Speaking as someone fiercely territorial, I've found that constantly defending my personal space was exhausting. No wonder my first editor — the late Owen McNamara in Boston in the early 1970s — wrote his weekly editorials from the sanctity of his own den, and that was well before open offices took hold.

By the time the Bond Buyer's parent company shoved everyone into the 27th floor on 1 State Street Plaza in Lower Manhattan — downsizing from three floors to one over time — I knew all too well the pitfalls of open space. Newsrooms generally had those layouts. As the sports editor of the Daily Freeman in Kingston, New York, for example, I had to frequently shut off the big television adjacent to the sports desk to fend off press-operator cretins who treated my work area as a sports bar, not to mention a wildly immature city editor who would turn on the Weather Channel at the drop of a snowflake and yell at the forecasters. I kept the remote in my briefcase and took it home every night. I still have it as a souvenir. As a news-desk editor at the Daily Record in Parsippany, New Jersey, I lobbied to confine telecasts of baseball playoff games on newsroom TVs to the sports department to minimize disruptive cheering and to "keep the blight from spreading."

At the Bond Buyer, adjustments to open office included speaking in code near our work areas and talking in whispered tones down the corridors and in the coffee room. My end-row seat put me near an open area where people often hollered on cellphones. Reserving conference rooms was a problem, especially with squatters that included people high on the corporate ladder. And within our department, we had someone who didn't cover his sneezing and didn't give a damn about it.

The company tried to put on its best face. One multimedia person even shot footage at our workstations as part of a video for the annual meeting. He asked us to smile and wave. I ducked and ran despite two bad hips. Smile and wave? What are we, North Korea? The Jewelry Factory of Hackensack?

I even had to file a formal complaint against three millennials who had an extremely loud conversation about nightclubbing inches from my workstation. I'm no buzzkill, but play is play and work is work. I had just returned from a press conference by then-New York Mayor Bill de Blasio and hoped to get some work done. Dirty looks from me and even my placing a small wastebasket on the floor as a barrier accomplished nothing. I left to finish my workday at home, and in the elevator lobby, a co-worker said, "Hey, they were loud, weren't they?"

It turns out the three went to the editor-in-chief's boss and whined that I made them "uncomfortable." I got out front and filed a formal complaint against the trio. The human-resources representative was dismissive. "It's open office, so you have to get used to it," she told me. HR people exist merely to defend the company. Stunningly, she also told me the manner in which I placed the wastebasket — whether I put it down too hard — may have constituted a hostile act. (Insert eyeroll here.)

While effective workplace communication is a must, the kind of fake dog-and-pony "collaboration" you see all too often today is just make-work. Many of us don't have time for that.

Former Pittsburgh Mayor Bill Peduto once told me how he likes to keep it simple. "My committee is a committee of one … me," he said. "I don't do blue ribbon. Blue-ribbon panels sit around and recommend things, then someone issues a report, and five years later nothing gets done."

Bingo.

"We live in the age of collaboration, in which the modest luxury of cubicles has been supplanted by open-plan offices, and technology offers a multitude of options to constantly converse with peers," Margery Weinstein wrote in Training magazine. "But the thing is, I'm not into collaboration, at least not the way many people define it. If collaboration means a lack of privacy — so that a small cubicle is too much to ask for — and those you're 'collaborating' with don't have to do any work — then count me out.

"I've found in my own work and life that what the group comes up with will be inferior to what the individual dreams up," Weinstein added.

Teamwork platitudes aside, most of us are in it for ourselves. To quote Sarah Stiles' character Bonnie Barella on the Wall Street–themed HBO drama "Billions": "If I want team spirit, I will work for fucking Chick-fil-A."

Collaboration also creates a trade deficit of sorts. I would sometimes contribute good material, say, to someone else's 50-inch article about education, but the other party would never reciprocate. "In most cases, 20% to 35% of value-added collaborations come from only 3% to 5% of employees," Bernstein and Waber wrote.

In short, some of us don't want others dragging us down.

At the Daily Freeman, one of my writers was working on a blockbuster story about bureaucratic nightmares local high-school athletes were having with the National Collegiate Athletic Association bureaucracy. An "NCAA clearinghouse," intended to screen academic workloads to ensure that athletes' high school courses weren't bogus, was an operational shitstorm. The writer, Mike Stribl, was onto something. Athletes' college scholarships were on hold over the silliest of reasons, often unrelated to course merits. Stribl, assistant sports editor Ron Rosner and I kept the developments under wraps for months from the news-side people, including a histrionic education reporter. This was the sports department's story.

We ran a four-part series for which Stribl won first place in a New York State contest for special enterprise reporting. Collaboration would have watered down the package. The award happened under my watch, so it became a conversation piece at interviews when I went job hunting after news broke of the Freeman's pending sale. "I fostered enterprise coverage" was my favorite line.

While we may not be able to fully ditch open-plan layouts, companies are evolving, especially post-pandemic.

"This means free-standing individual work pods are in, as well as computer screens that wrap around, affording the worker more privacy," David Levitt wrote in the Commercial Observer. "Out are somewhat cornier items once thought to create a fun office environment."

Christine Congdon, director of global research communications for office furniture manufacturer and seller Steelcase, told Levitt the company's business strategy is evolving.

"The jury is still out in terms of what's out," she said. "But I would say things that are kind of frivolous [are out]. Things that the organizations maybe picked up from the dot-com companies and thought, 'If I only put a slide or a foosball table in my office, then it would be cool.' That's clearly been rejected by employees."

All hope is not lost. As Levitt wrote, "Maybe Clark Kent has a place to change into Superman after all."

Dumb jocks no more

Takeaways from a background in sports

Moments before the Boston Red Sox set out to complete their historic comeback in 2004 against the New York Yankees, winning the last four games of the American League Championship Series after losing the first three, ESPN's Dan Patrick referenced "compelling theater" at Yankee Stadium.

Actor, activist and New York sports fan Spike Lee cut him off. "Movies, that stuff's fake," Lee said. "That's why sports is the greatest because it can't be scripted."

Sports forces you to improvise. "People with backgrounds in sports and crime adapt well to other kinds of writing," a colleague told me late in my career. "They have a knack for drama. You can't script it, and you have to be quick on your feet." For example, dozens of sportswriters at New York's Shea Stadium in October 1986 had to hurriedly rework their lead paragraphs on deadline after the Mets, four times a strike away from losing the Word Series, rallied to deny the Red Sox their first title since 1918.

When I was a senior editor at mergers-and-acquisitions-oriented The Deal, one of our best bankruptcy reporters, Terry Brennan, was a veteran of crime-beat coverage in Philadelphia. He was streetwise in a way many of our younger writers there were not.

Sports coverage today often involves gambling legislation, judicial rulings, labor law, salary-cap maneuvering, pandemic policies and franchise relocation … much of it wrapped in politics. Sports often overflowed into public finance. Our coverage of Major League Baseball's sweeping reorganization of its minor-league system, which it charted right before COVID-19 escalated, cited widespread repercussions for the economies of many smaller communities nationwide. Cities that lost franchises had to figure out how to pay for taxpayer-backed stadiums that they funded on the assumed basis of a long-term stay.

"The reach and expectations of sports journalism have expanded in recent years," St. Bonaventure University said as it plugged its media programs on its website. "Previous generations expected box scores and highlights from their newspapers, radio shows and TV stations. Sports reporting now tells stories at the intersection of society and athletics using a wide variety of media."

And, the school emphasized, sports journalism has no offseason. "Around-the-clock access to sports news and social media has raised expectations of full-year coverage. The question for sports writers and sports editors is how to fill months without games, transactions, or drafts." That, of course, means we're subjected to trade rumors and "mock drafts" ad nauseam, notably around the National Football League draft every spring. Even the NFL schedule release in 2022 came incrementally — international games, highlighted games and first home-opponent games before the full slate, in what the Kansas City Chiefs fan website Arrowhead Pride called "the ol' announcement-about-an-announcement trick."

The pandemic hit sports especially hard, with cities scurrying to replace lost revenue from the cancellation of sporting events. One-horse college towns were especially vulnerable. Tom Kozlik of investment firm Hilltop Securities said in one commentary that annual football-related revenue in places like State College, Pennsylvania, and Columbus, Ohio, was the equivalent of "five or six Christmases."

My award-winning Future of Cities podcast series for the Bond Buyer covered a range of pandemic-related sports topics, from the future of gambling mecca Las Vegas to the effects of youth sports travel teams on roadside communities such as Williamsport, Pennsylvania, home to the annual Little League World Series.

"This crisis has affected every job everywhere in sports," said Bob Boland, a former Penn State University law professor and former player agent, now at Seton Hall Law School.

Sports, meanwhile, helped propel many business and political careers. Bill Bradley was a basketball All-American at Princeton and a Rhodes Scholar who became a U.S. senator from New Jersey and a presidential candidate. Future president Gerald Ford was a football star at the University of Michigan. George H.W. Bush, three presidents after Ford, was a standout at Yale University, playing in college baseball's World Series.

Phil McConkey, en route to the presidency of military veteran-oriented investment firm Academy Securities, had to survive the rigors of the Naval Academy and playing for one of pro football's toughest coaches, Bill Parcells.

He recalled scratching his cornea in the New York Giants training camp. After seeing a doctor during the midday break, McConkey returned for the afternoon session. Under Parcells, you didn't dare miss it.

McConkey, patch over one eye like Sinbad, caught passes and punts. "I had no depth perception." The ball slipped out of McConkey's hands during the final punt.

"This SOB yelled and screamed at me as if I had just fumbled away the Super Bowl. No matter how well I did, he would critique and complain and bitch," McConkey said of Parcells. "The man was absolute. He refused to accept excuses."

McConkey drew on that experience. "Having no excuses teaches you to get more out of yourself."

He went on to a successful NFL career that included a touchdown reception in the Giants' 39-20 Super Bowl victory over the Denver Broncos in January 1987. Still, he regretted the possible 60-yard touchdown toss that didn't materialize that day because a defender interfered. Likewise, Navy beat Army three of four times while McConkey was at Annapolis, but the memory of losing to the Black Knights his junior year still stung.

"I hated losing a hell of a lot more than I enjoyed winning," he told me in a Bond Buyer interview. "When I was a Wall Street trader, I made some great trades, but some of the ones that got away still bother me."

When McConkey arrived at the Naval Academy as "a skinny kid from Buffalo," he thought frequently about leaving Annapolis. "Every day I hated the place."

McConkey persevered and co-captained the football team his senior year. After graduation, he worked for five years as a naval aviator and nuclear weapons transshipment pilot.

"In high school they gave you multiple-choice exams, and if you didn't know the answer, you could guess and pick answer C," he said. "On a fighter plane you have to do 10 things at once off memorization, and there's no bull-shitting that. You either do or you don't."

McConkey also won two New York Sports Emmy awards analyzing the Giants on local TV. The lobby of the KeyBank Center in downtown Buffalo has a tribute to McConkey, whom the Buffalo Sports Hall of Fame inducted in 2013.

Twice in my own career as a sports editor, Game 7 of the World Series went into extra innings, forcing me to think of alternate headlines and photos to use under an instant turnaround. You had to think of "Twins win" and "Braves win" scenarios, and in the predigital "pasteup board" days of newsrooms, you had to measure headline length in advance.

Variables included color photos, and back then, if you had color, you had to commit to it early. Using an early celebration shot was risky because the other team might come back and win. When I was the sports editor in Kingston, New York, I changed my plans for color usage during the 1997 World Series, scrapping a Cleveland celebration shot in Game 3 after the Florida Marlins overcame a 7-3 sixth-inning deficit and won 14-11. For Game 7 the rival Middletown Times Herald-Record used a color photo of two Cleveland players high-fiving each other early in the game. Yet Florida came back to win in the 11th inning. Oops.

The sports department's use of processed color in Kingston was limited at the time. Unfortunate in the big picture, but at times a blessing. Switching black-and-white photos for later editions was much easier. That enabled me to run in our final edition a photo of Toronto Blue Jays outfielder Joe Carter celebrating his World Series–ending home run in 1993.

Even in nondaily situations, you had to come up with a Plan B, akin to a "checkdown" in football where a quarterback throws short to a safety-valve receiver when the deep wideout can't get open. As editor-in-chief of biweekly Hartford Sports Extra in the late 1980s, and doubling as the magazine's NHL columnist, I had a huge spread in the making about the upcoming Stanley Cup playoffs, predicated on the hometown Whalers finishing first and facing the Quebec Nordiques in the first round. Yet Hartford came perilously close to blowing the division title and playing the Boston Bruins instead. I had Plan B, a form of "organized chaos" if you will, in place. Luckily the Whalers held on, though they exited in the first round of the playoffs. Their demise prompted my one-word main headline: "Splat!"

I spent much of the first half of my career as a sports editor, editor-in-chief of a sports magazine, traveling NHL columnist and a local-level radio and TV play-by-play announcer. Return trips to Boston Garden to cover the Whalers often felt surreal. I grew up as a "Garden rat," and suddenly I was there in a jacket and tie with people referring to me as "out-of-town media."

My effort to get out of sports — working too many nights and weekends put me in a different time zone from the rest of the world — was difficult given the "dumb jock" inferences while job-hunting. At one company I applied internally for an administrative position, wanting to leave my dead-end gig as a sports editor of a chain of community weeklies. "We were nonplussed," the executive editor told me, tone paternalistic.

Unfortunately, we're still a society of stereotypes. One former colleague had trouble shaking the "lifestyle" label — inferring a person of leisure — before she landed an excellent gig designing front pages for the Hartford Courant. At one place I worked, some yuppie ad-sales rep suggested I was a "man without a country" with NFL players on strike. I laughed in his face. Years later, when I volunteered for my newspaper's spelling-bee team, the news editor said, only half-jokingly, that maybe they didn't want jocks on the team. I persisted and earned a spot. We didn't do well in the competition, but I made my point.

Trust me, too many game stories on daily deadline can make you loopy. Many top writers across the country have tried to work columns and commentaries into their job descriptions for that reason. Back when sports departments had better funding, they often succeeded in getting editors to assign other people to game stories.

I largely avoided "beat writers" when I took over at Hartford Sports Extra and had a pool of freelancers at my disposal. Some beat writers were great people, mind you, but I needed creativity, not verbal hackdom. I brought in those who delivered for me elsewhere and knew what I wanted. "Paul Burton was the most demanding editor I worked for, but I liked working for him because if you put out for him, he stood behind you," said one of my former writers. "And Paul communicates."

As a sports editor, the frequent grind of putting out multiple editions, deadlines and all, can wear you down. That's why doing things differently refreshes you. Creativity in any business invigorates the brain.

The growth of female sports over the past generation also posed challenges. There was much more to cover, frequently with less staff at your disposal. Sometimes college women's and high school girls' sports made for the better story on a given day, even with attendance frequently low at their events. You had to factor that into judgment calls as a sports editor. Enterprise coverage options included better pay or better facilities for female athletes and initiatives to shatter the "glass ceiling," such as coaching positions in baseball.

Over time my sports background became a beneficial conversation piece. Many finance professionals were sports fans, too, which helped with networking. Some of my news sources played college club hockey, minor-league baseball or women's collegiate rugby.

Kim Magrini, a public-finance attorney with Ballard Spahr in Philadelphia, said the teamwork necessary as a rugby player at Penn

State applied to her professional career. "The interesting aspect of public finance as a legal field is that you work with different people," she told me. Rugby itself is an improv sport. She played a position called scrum half, which she likened to a point guard in basketball. "There are no timeouts, and the coach doesn't call all the plays like in football," she said.

"A player makes the decisions along with 14 teammates, and you have to analyze the other side as well."